MIND TRAINER

THE BRAIN TEASER BOOK

# MIND TRAINER
# THE
# BRAIN TEASER BOOK

JAKE OLEFSKY

D&C
David and Charles

A DAVID & CHARLES BOOK
Copyright © David & Charles Limited 2009

David & Charles is an F+W Media Inc. company
4700 East Galbraith Road
Cincinnati, OH 45236

First published in the USA in 2006 as *The Everything Brain Strain Book*
This paperback edition first published in the UK in 2009

Jake Olefsky has asserted his right to be identified as author of this work
in accordance with the Copyright, Designs and Patents Act, 1988.

ISBN-13: 978-0-7153-3621-2
ISBN-10: 0-7153-3621-5

Printed in the UK by CPI Cox & Wyman
for David & Charles
Brunel House    Newton Abbot    Devon


Visit our website at www.davidandcharles.co.uk

David & Charles books are available from all good bookshops; alternatively you
can contact our Orderline on 0870 9908222 or write to us at FREEPOST EX2 110,
D&C Direct, Newton Abbot, TQ12 4ZZ (no stamp required UK only); US customers
call 800-289-0963 and Canadian customers call 800-840-5220.

## EDITORIAL

Publishing Director: Gary M. Krebs
Managing Editor: Kate McBride
Copy Chief: Laura M. Daly
Acquisitions Editor: Gina Chaimanis
Development Editor: Christina MacDonald
Production Editors: Jamie Wielgus, Bridget Brace

## PRODUCTION

Production Director: Susan Beale
Production Manager: Michelle Roy Kelly
Series Designer: Daria Perreault
Cover Design: Paul Beatrice and Matt LeBlanc
Layout and Graphics: Colleen Cunningham,
Daria Perreault, Erin Ring

# Acknowledgments

I'd like to thank my family for their support – especially my wife, for being such a good brain-teaser tester.

I would also like to thank all of the users of Braingle.com who provided me with the inspiration to write this book. Special thanks to users Bobbrt and Mad-Ade, who contributed some of their own puzzles to this book.

# Contents

# **Introduction**

***Many people enjoy solving brain-teasers.*** For some, the satisfaction comes from figuring out the solution to a difficult puzzle. For others it's just the entertainment derived from the amusing stories and clever answers that accompany a good brain-teaser. Whatever the reason, it is clear that brain-teasers have been popular for thousands of years. The earliest known form of brain-teaser is probably the tangram, an ancient Chinese puzzle of seven pieces that fit together in different ways to form a variety of shapes. There are also records of puzzles written on the walls of pyramids and temples around the world.

There are more benefits to solving brain-teasers than just plain fun. Several medical benefits come from solving puzzles. People who solve brain-teasers have been shown to experience a delayed onset of Alzheimer's compared to people who do not exercise their brains. In addition, keeping your mind in tiptop shape will boost your creativity and mental flexibility. This is why many top design firms use brain-teasers as part of their daily routines. People exercise to keep their bodies physically fit, so why shouldn't they also perform exercises to keep their minds mentally fit? Solving puzzles is one way to keep your mind in peak condition.

Just like physical exercise, where you do different movements to work out different parts of the body, you should do different types of mental exercise to work out different parts of your brain. The various chapters in this book contain many different types of puzzles, some based on maths and some on language. Flip through the pages, and try out some of each. Maths and language brain-teasers stretch different parts of your brain, and some people are naturally better at one particular type of puzzle than another. You probably already know your favourite kind of puzzle, but you shouldn't avoid the other types. This is probably the part of your mind that needs the most exercise. With a little practice, you will surely get better. Just start out with the easier puzzles in that chapter, and work up from there.

You've surely heard the phrase, "Two minds are better than one." It's true. Brain-teasers are great for sharing with friends, especially if you're stumped on a particularly difficult puzzle. Instead of flipping straight to the answer, why not try to work it out with a friend? You'll be amazed at how much more quickly you can solve puzzles when you have someone helping you. It's no surprise that brain-teasers are great group activities. Just look at how many popular board games have some form of puzzle as their main element. There's something about solving a difficult problem as a group that brings everybody closer together.

Whatever your reason for enjoying brain-teasers, the rest of this book is sure to be a pleasure for you to read. Have fun!

## Chapter 1
# Quickie Teasers

These teasers are all nice and easy. Think of them as appetisers for the rest of the book. If you can solve these in under a minute each, then you are ready to dive into the other chapters. The kinds of puzzles contained in the different chapters are all represented by at least one of these quickies.

### Quickie Teaser 1

This is a rebus teaser. A common phrase is disguised by using the placement and orientation of letters as clues. What is this phrase?

PEACE
EARTH

### Quickie Teaser 2

Here's another rebus:

JUMPING
JOY
JOY
JOY
JOY

## Alert!

If any of these quickies is taking you longer than 10 minutes to solve, stop. Try a different brain-teaser and come back to the difficult one later. Sometimes you just need to approach the puzzle from a different direction.

### Quickie Teaser 3

In this group teaser, once you work out the rule, name another word that also belongs in the group.

KAYAK, TENET, MOM, DEED

## Quickie Teaser 4

This is a group teaser. Your challenge is to work out the rule for words that can be included in a particular group. This rule may have something to do with the items that the words represent or with the letters in the words themselves. Which of the following does not belong in this group?

CHEESE, CORN, CRANBERRIES,
CARROTS, CAULIFLOWER

## Quickie Teaser 5

This is a letter-equation teaser. This is a well-known fact or phrase where the key words have been replaced by the first letter of that word. Can you work out what the letters stand for?

24 H = 1 D

## Quickie Teaser 6

Here's another letter equation:

S W and the 7 D

## Quickie Teaser 7

A swimmer jumps into an Olympic-size swimming pool and does one lap before getting out completely dry. How is this possible?

## Quickie Teaser 8

You have a fuse that is 10 feet long. You know that this fuse burns at a rate of 1 foot per minute. How can you burn the entire fuse in five minutes?

## Quickie Teaser 9

A father and his son are taking a walk. The father notices that his shadow is 15 feet long. He knows that he is 5 feet tall and that his son is 2 feet tall. How long is the son's shadow?

## Quickie Teaser 10

You see a basket containing 23 apples. You take seven of them, decide you want more, and take half of what's left. Then you decide that you took too many apples, so you put back one third of what you have. How many apples are in the basket?

## Quickie Teaser 11

What is one half of one quarter of one tenth of 80?

## Quickie Teaser 12

Bobby Braingle has a dog named Sparky and a cat named Snowball. Sparky is twelve years old. Snowball is seven years old. How many years ago was Sparky twice as old as Snowball?

## Quickie Teaser 13

There is a four-digit number in which the second digit is one less than the first digit, the third digit is half the second digit, and the fourth digit is three less than the third digit. The second digit is even, and the fourth digit is odd. What is the number?

## Quickie Teaser 14

Bobby Braingle flips a standard coin 10 times, and remarkably it comes up heads all 10 times. What is the probability that it will come up heads an eleventh time?

## Quickie Teaser 15

Bobby is stacking cans of soup on the shelf at the local grocery store. When he comes to the bottom of his box, he notices that the labels have come off four of the cans. All four labels are different. If Bobby reattaches the labels at random, what is the probability that he will have correctly labelled three of the cans?

## Quickie Teaser 16

How would you turn a straight piece of dry spaghetti into a circular piece of dry spaghetti?

## Quickie Teaser 17

What is the next number in this series?

1, 4, 16, 64, 256, ?

### Quickie Teaser 18
Which does not belong?

W, SE, NW, E, N, SN, NE

### Quickie Teaser 19
You are at the North Pole. Put on a blindfold, and spin around two times. Take 10 steps forward, and turn 90 degrees to the left. What do you see?

### Quickie Teaser 20
What is next in this series?

H, He, Li, Be, B, C, N, O , ?

### Quickie Teaser 21
Dihydrogen monoxide can corrode metals and will kill you if you inhale enough of it. It's a leading component of acid rain and is used in many industrial chemical plants. Surprisingly, it's also a key ingredient in most sodas. How can this be?

### Quickie Teaser 22
Would you rather have £5 million all at once or have someone give you 1p and then double it each day for a month?

### Quickie Teaser 23
Karin has two dolls. One is very expensive and costs £100 more than the cheap one. Both dolls together cost £101. How much does each doll cost?

## Quickie Teaser 24
Your mother's brother's brother-in-law gives you a present. You have no aunts. Who gave you the present?

## Quickie Teaser 25
You and your sister are trying to decide who gets the last cookie in the cookie jar. Your sister proposes this contest: roll a die; you get the number facing up and she gets the number facing down. The higher number wins. Whoever wins two out of three rounds gets the cookie. Should you take this bet?

## Quickie Teaser 26
What has leaves without branches?

## Quickie Teaser 27
Cheese is to a cow as flour is to what?

a. Wheat
b. Bread
c. Grass
d. Moo

## Quickie Teaser 28

What is the next letter in this sequence?

O, T, T, F, F, S, S, ?

## *Fact*

For more brain-teasers, check out *www.braingle.com*. On this web site you can browse more than 7,000 brain-teasers by category or difficulty. If you feel up to it, you can also submit your own brain-teaser for inclusion on the web site. You can also join an active community of brain-teaser enthusiasts to participate in message boards and games.

## Chapter 2
# Group Teasers

These brain-teasers rely on your ability to recognize groups of common attributes. For each of these puzzles you'll need to work out why the words or letters are grouped as they are. Sometimes you will be asked to pick the odd one out or to add a new word to the correct group.

## Group Teaser 1

△ Difficulty: medium

Which of these letter groups does not belong?

YUI, SDF, VBN, ERT, GLK

## Group Teaser 2

△ Difficulty: easy

Why have these letters been divided into these two groups?

1. TNLKAZY
2. RQOJGDS

## Group Teaser 3

△ Difficulty: medium

Which sentence does not belong?

1. Alice prefers pink letter envelopes.
2. Ben always needs a new aspirin.
3. Ken is with Isabel.
4. Sally has twelve blue igloos.

## Group Teaser 4

 Difficulty: hard

One word in Group 1 belongs in Group 2, and vice versa. Can you work out which words need to be swapped?

1. HEAR, UNDER, BREAD, ELEVEN
2. INKS, READ, EATER, TEE

## Group Teaser 5

 Difficulty: easy

What do the following words have in common?

RESET, TREE, SEAT, STEER, EARS

## Group Teaser 6

 Difficulty: medium

The letters of the alphabet have been sorted into two groups. In which group would you place the letter J?

1. GPQY
2. ABCDEFHIKLMNORSTUVWXZ

## Group Teaser 7

⚠ Difficulty: medium

What other word would fit in this group?

LISTEN, SILENT, TINSEL, INLETS

## Group Teaser 8

⚠ Difficulty: easy

In which group would you place the letter Q?

1. CWSMKZ
2. DARPOB

## Group Teaser 9

⚠ Difficulty: hard

What do the following states (listed alphabetically) have in common?

| | |
|---|---|
| Alaska | Minnesota |
| Arizona | New Hampshire |
| California | New Mexico |
| Connecticut | Oregon |
| Hawaii | South Dakota |
| Illinois | Texas |
| Kentucky | Washington |
| Maine | |

## Group Teaser 10

 Difficulty: hard

The following words are related in some way. Can you work out how?

ENOUGH, BLOWTORCH, MARXIST, MENINGITIS, NETTLE

## Group Teaser 11

 Difficulty: medium

Which of the following words does not belong?

ANT, WEAK, ROAD, PAUSE, CHEESE, BERRY

## Group Teaser 12

 Difficulty: easy

Here are five words that belong together:

CAFÉ, CABBAGE, GABBED, CAGED, BADGE

Which one of the following words also belongs?

BEEF, CHICKEN, GOURD, FABLE

### Group Teaser 13

⚠ Difficulty: hard

What do the following words have in common?

CONQUERED, ALSO, FRONT, DEVOURED, ATTACKS

### Group Teaser 14

⚠ Difficulty: medium

Bobby Braingle has accidentally knocked over his in-tray and his out-tray. Eight pieces of paper have fallen onto the floor, each with a single word printed on it. Can you work out which of the following words belong in Bobby's inbox and which belong in his outbox?

JURY, LINE, BACK, TENT, BURST,
VOICE, TENSE, CRY

### Group Teaser 15

⚠ Difficulty: easy

What do the following have in common?

CSBLNC
THGDFTHR
THWZRDFOZ
TSWNDRFLLF

## Group Teaser 16

 Difficulty: easy

Where would you be most likely to find the following?

ALOLRIG, EFRGAFI, EETAHLNP,
HECTAEH, THISCOR

## Group Teaser 17

 Difficulty: medium

On a busy night at a wedding chapel in Las Vegas, four marriages were performed. Unfortunately, the marriage certificate for the fourth marriage was lost. The officials know that the groom's name is Steve, but they can't remember if his bride is Eve, Jill, or Kathy. Can you figure which girl is Steve's bride?

1. Frank married Alice.
2. Bob married Cynthia.
3. Jeff married Maggie.
4. Steve married ?

## Group Teaser 18

 Difficulty: hard

One of the following letter combinations does not belong. Which one is it?

Eu, Sm, Pr, Ho, Hg, Yb, Ce

### Group Teaser 19

 Difficulty: easy

Which number does not belong?

12, 13, 14, 15, 16

## *Essential*

Here are a few things to consider when you're trying to work out the grouping of a bunch of letters. Which numbers in the alphabet are the letters? How are the letters drawn, typed, pronounced? What happens if you rearrange some of the letters?

### Group Teaser 20

 Difficulty: hard

What is so special about these letters?

D, D, P, V, C, C, D, B

### Group Teaser 21

 Difficulty: easy

Adam, Isabel, and Eric each own a dog. Jane, Joshua, and Chloe each own a cat. Which kind of pet owner would Emma be?

## Group Teaser 22

 Difficulty: medium

The following words have been placed in this order for a reason. What is it?

Trick
Squad
Serpent
Cathexis
Antiseptic
Octopus

## Group Teaser 23

 Difficulty: hard

The letters of the alphabet have been split into two groups. In which group would you put the letter Z?

1. AEFHIJLPRSUVW
2. BCDGKMNOQTXY

## Group Teaser 24

 Difficulty: easy

The following letters have a unique relationship that none of the other letters in the alphabet shares. Can you guess what it is?

CDILMVX

## Group Teaser 25

 Difficulty: medium

Oberon and Titania went to the toy shop to buy their niece Ariel a birthday present. A helpful shop assistant named Rosalind helped them select a picture-book entitled *Cordelia Goes to the Beach*. When they got home, they phoned Ariel's mother, Portia, to make sure Ariel didn't already have this book. Unfortunately, she had already been given a copy for Christmas, so Oberon and Titania went back to the shop. This time, an assistant named Belinda helped them select a different book. Which book did they select?

1. *Sammy the Snake Eats a Cake*
2. *Bianca Bubbles Buys a Balloon*
3. *Martha Has a Pet Monkey*
4. *Lysander Tells a White Lie*

## Group Teaser 26

 Difficulty: easy

What other name would fit into this group?

George, John, James, Andrew, William

## Group Teaser 27

 Difficulty: hard

The following numbers are all related in some way. Can you figure it out?

39.37
3.281
1.0936
0.00062

## Fact

Here's another tip for solving group teasers. Look at the letters themselves. How many letters are in each word? How many vowels or consonants are there? Can you add or take away certain letters to form a pattern?

## Group Teaser 28

 Difficulty: medium

The following countries are grouped together for a specific reason. Which other country belongs in this exclusive group?

ALGERIA, BURKINA FASO, FRANCE,
GHANA, MALI, SPAIN, UNITED KINGDOM

## Group Teaser 29

 Difficulty: easy

Which word does not belong?

    DEAD, RED, BLEED, SAID, DREAD

## Group Teaser 30

 Difficulty: hard

Shannon's favourite dessert is apple pie. Tom's favourite dessert is fudge. Isabella's favourite dessert is dark-chocolate ice cream. Which of the following is Debbie's favourite dessert?

a. Strawberries and cream
b. Flan
c. Candy bars

## *Chapter 3*
# Language Teasers

L anguage brain-teasers play on the English language. These types of puzzles require you to manipulate words, rearrange letters, know definitions, and generally be good at linguistics.

## Language Teaser 1

 Difficulty: easy

Below are four epitaphs that appear on some fictional gravestones. From the writings, can you work out the occupation of each person?

1. Here lies Mortimer Bibbs. He took part of ours and gave it to big brother, but he always had good form.
2. Here lies Dirk McDuff, who toppled giants with weapons of steel. If only he'd heard his partner's shout before the giants found their revenge.
3. Here lies Suzy Smelt. She constructed many a bomb but mostly brought smiles to our faces.
4. Here lies Ethel Grant. She spent her whole life fighting with what she will now become.

## Language Teaser 2

 Difficulty: easy

In the following sentence, fill in the blanks with words that are the same except for their first letters.

My _____, the _____, would _____ _____ with soap than with body wash.

## Language Teaser 3

 Difficulty: easy

The blanks in these sentences will be filled in with three different homonyms (words that sound alike but are spelled differently) to make valid sentences. The dashes indicate the number of letters in the words. Can you fill in the blanks?

1. The cut on his _ _ _ _ won't _ _ _ _ in time for the race, so _ _ ' _ _ have to drop out.
2. The man was so upset about being _ _ _ _ that he regularly _ _ _ _ _ _ himself up on the bed and _ _ _ _ _ _ his eyes out.
3. A pirate will wander the _ _ _ _ and essentially _ _ _ _ _ everything he _ _ _ _.

## Language Teaser 4

 Difficulty: medium

Below are two clues for words that are homonyms. For example, "Number after one . . . Also" would result in "Two . . . Too." Can you get all of the words?

1. Tiny spider . . . Not sure if I will or not
2. Made the gun more accurate . . . Quoted
3. Prophet . . . Scorch
4. Container . . . Light
5. Head organ . . . Yes

## Language Teaser 5

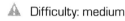 Difficulty: medium

For each group below, fill in the blanks with two words that differ only by their first letters.

1. Stop thinking over here. Go _ _ _ _ _ _ over _ _ _ _ _ _.
2. An untrained person could be killed in these woods, but there is little _ _ _ _ _ _ for a _ _ _ _ _ _.
3. Writing an "A" on your dishrag would make it a _ _ _ _ _ with a _ _ _ _ _.

## Language Teaser 6

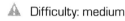 Difficulty: medium

The following five clues describe five different spoonerisms (pairs of words with their initial sounds switched). Can you figure them all out?

1. Battling a fibber . . . Igniting the charcoal
2. Not enough pastries . . . Many untruths
3. Angry rabbit . . . Counterfeit bills
4. Bathe standing up . . . What an earthquake in Pisa does
5. Physically rude panther . . . Adoring lamb-keeper

## Language Teaser 7

 Difficulty: hard

Each clue below describes two words that differ by only one letter. The extra letter has been either added to the beginning or the end of the second word – all the rest are in the same order. For example "Writing on the wall of Noah's boat" would result in "Ark mark." Can you get the rest?

1. Complaint about a golf-club part
2. Insect being angry and vocal
3. Angry buccaneer
4. The second of the two dishes
5. Scrawny unidentified object

## Language Teaser 8

 Difficulty: easy

The following are alternate definitions for words, based on how the words sound. For example, "To drive by the docks" would be an alternate definition for PASSPORT (pass port). Can you guess the rest of the words described below?

1. What white bears see with: P _ _ _ _ _ _ _
2. A car's memoirs: A _ _ _ _ _ _ _ _ _ _ _
3. How judges get across the ocean: C _ _ _ _ _ _ _ _
4. To live long: D _ _ _ _ _
5. A knack for fibbing: L _ _ _ _ _ _ _

## Language Teaser 9

⚠ Difficulty: medium

Below are two clues for words that are homonyms (same sound but different spelling). Can you get all of the words?

1. Uninterested . . . panel
2. Permitted . . . spoken
3. Walked . . . adhesive
4. Cries for help . . . satisfy
5. Small bag . . . strut or flounce

## Language Teaser 10

⚠ Difficulty: medium

Use the clue to work out what two smaller words will combine to make one compound word. For example: Elevated + Easy to carry = Highlight (high + light)

1. Not over + Not sit = ?
2. Not tall + Slice or divide = ?
3. Large four-legged animal + Foot protection = ?
4. Hot beverage + Eating utensil = ?
5. Natural sweet substance + Planetary satellite = ?

## Language Teaser 11

⚠ Difficulty: medium

Here are some more compound word puzzles. Use the clues to work out which two smaller words will fit together to make one compound word.

1. Clear liquid + Plummet = ?
2. Something to read + Type of container = ?
3. Celestial body + Swimming animal = ?
4. Head topping + Piece of furniture = ?
5. Sandwich spread + Whisky = ?

## Language Teaser 12

⚠ Difficulty: easy

The following are alternate definitions for words, based on how the words sound. Can you guess the rest of the words described below?

1. A laid-back play:
   M _ _ _ _ _ _ _ _.
2. Grief over not shooting a birdie:
   P _ _ _ _ _ _ _ _.
3. Happening in winter, summer, or fall:
   O _ _ _ _ _ _ _.
4. Where a carpenter stands when building a floor:
   O _ _ _ _ _ _ _.

## Language Teaser 13

 Difficulty: easy

Fill in each blank with the same letters, in the same order, to complete the following sentence. The first letter or letters of each word are provided. The dashes tell you how many letters are missing.

During the baseball game, the CH_ _ _ _ _ didn't bother the L_ _ _ _ _ B_ _ _ _ _, but it did bother the one before him.

## Language Teaser 14

Difficulty: medium

Here are some definitions for a few words. The number of letters in each word is given in parentheses. Each definition is followed by a clue to a split-apart version of the answer. For "Pondering (8) . . . Monarch after dieting," the answer would be THINKING (with the clue leading you to the split-apart version, "thin king").

1. Certain evening (9) . . . Tiny chess piece
2. Deed subjects (10) . . . Cravats that are suitable
3. Ne'er-do-well (11) . . . Onion that performs hip-hop music
4. Hawaiian person, for instance (8) . . . Confession of a scandalmonger
5. Buddhist belief (13) . . . Flower adorning a horse's bridle

## Language Teaser 15

 Difficulty: hard

Each of the following clues is for a pair of palindromes. In this case, you read the first word backward to get the other word. Can you work out all four?

1. Part of a caribou's clarinet
2. The king's beer
3. Moisturizer for your calves
4. A malicious stare at one's fishing tackle

## Language Teaser 16

 Difficulty: hard

The words in the following list are out of order. Can you work out the pattern (which is NOT alphabetical) and put them in the proper order?

a. Leaf
b. Part
c. Mitt
d. Corn
e. Saw

## Language Teaser 17

⚠ Difficulty: easy

Fill in the blanks in the following sentences with rhyming words.

1. The _ _ _ _ _ _ _ _ of a traffic light is to make a road
   _ _ _ _ _ _ _ _ safer.
2. Like the saying goes, you can't _ _ _ _ _ a _ _ _ _ _
   to drink. He'll do it in due _ _ _ _ _ _.
3. The _ _ _ _ _ _ was terrible at _ _ _ _ _ _ because
   he was much too short and kept slipping on the ice.

## Language Teaser 18

⚠ Difficulty: easy

Below are clues to words that start with the prefix "man."
Can you work out the words?

1. Cuffs: _ _ _ _ _ _ _ _
2. Sea cow: _ _ _ _ _ _ _
3. Command: _ _ _ _ _ _ _
4. Dummy: _ _ _ _ _ _ _ _ _
5. Guide: _ _ _ _ _ _

## Language Teaser 19

⚠ Difficulty: medium

You'll need to mix things up twice to solve this puzzle. Each word on the left can be scrambled and used to fill in the blanks in one of the words on the right to make a new word. For example, you would scramble "Lot" to fill in "S _ _ _ E N" and make the word "STOLEN." Can you work out which word goes where?

a. Access
b. Strain
c. Staged
d. Pretty
e. Slates

1. D I _ A _ V _ N _ A _ _
2. _ O M _ R _ _ U _ _
3. _ _ N I _ E N _ I A _ _
4. _ E _ _ _ _ E R _
5. _ _ _ R _ I T I _ _

## Language Teaser 20

⚠ Difficulty: hard

The following words, when modified according to the same general rule, will each fit one of the definitions listed below. Can you work out how to properly modify each word and then match it with the proper definition?

PICKLE, KNIGHT, CHOIR, TIRE, TREE, FIN, TENT

1. Peace-talks goal
2. Man's title
3. Fairylike
4. Join
5. High-pitched flute
6. Whole

## Language Teaser 21

⚠ Difficulty: medium

Each of the following is a clue to a word that can be formed by sounding out a shorter word and combining it with a letter of the alphabet, placed either before or after the word. The blanks indicate where to insert the extra letter. For example, "Aladdin's friend: _-_ _ _ _" is the clue for a word made by sounding out the letter "G" and following it by the word KNEE. The answer in this case would be GENIE. Can you figure them all out?

1. Fashionable: _ _ _ _ _ -_
2. Coerce: _ -_ _ _ _
3. Admiration: _ -_ _ _ _
4. Hold closely: _ -_ _ _ _ _
5. Flute's cousin: _ -_ _ _
6. Perchance: _ _ _ -_

## Language Teaser 22

⚠ Difficulty: easy

What palindrome will fit in the spaces below to make a complete sentence? Remember, a palindrome is the same whether you read it backward or forward. In this case, you need to find a whole phrase that makes a palindrome.

> Since you gained so much weight, your shoe doesn't fit any more. You must have _ _ _ _ _ _ _ _ _ _ _.

## Language Teaser 23

 Difficulty: medium

To find the answers to the following questions, you start with words that begin with the prefix "in." But the words will only answer the questions when a space is added after the "in." For example, the answer to the question "Where is the horse?" would be INSTALL (in stall). Obviously it's not proper grammar, but you get the point. Can you work out the "in" words that answer the following questions?

1. Where is my sleeping bag?
2. Where is my wife's stomach?
3. Where does the air go after the fan sucks it up?
4. I put some food down in the seabird's cage. Where did it go?
5. Where is the church bell?

## *Essential*

A homonym is a word that sounds and is often spelled the same as another word with a different meaning. An example would be "bear" (the animal) and "bear" (to carry).

## Language Teaser 24

⚠ Difficulty: medium

In their complete forms, each word in the list below includes the same letter at least three times. This letter has been removed, and the remaining letters are still in their proper order. For example, "oer" is TOTTER with all of the "Ts" removed. Can you determine the five words?

1. AAIN
2. FAIBE
3. EER
4. AEE
5. INIU

## Language Teaser 25

⚠ Difficulty: easy

The following is a list of made-up cartoon characters that are all appropriately named. For example, Bob would be a good name for a buoy (because a buoy bobs up and down). Can you get all of the names? The first letter of each is given. All are common American names.

1. R _ _ _ _ _ _ the Leaf
2. B _ _ _ the Nail
3. P _ _ _ _ _ the Hamburger
4. S _ _ _ _ the Beach
5. M _ _ _ the Pen
6. C _ _ _ _ _ the Basket

## Language Teaser 26

△ Difficulty: medium

In each of the following clues, a definition is given. Fill in the blanks with two rhyming words that fit the definition.

1. A T-bone for a pick-pocket: _ _ _ _ for a _ _ _ _ _
2. A fool with an open sore: A _ _ _ _ _ _ with a _ _ _ _ _ _
3. Don't stop the horse: Don't _ _ _ _ _ _ the _ _ _ _ _
4. Smart mousy creature: A _ _ _ _ _ with a _ _ _ _

## Language Teaser 27

△ Difficulty: hard

Each of the following words in the numbered list has a synonym that is a homonym of a synonym of a word in the lettered list. Sound complicated? Here's an example: BUCKET could link up with LIGHT, using the words PAIL and PALE.

Can you work out which words match below?

| | | |
|---|---|---|
| 1. Crimson | A. | Locale |
| 2. Elk | B. | Gawk |
| 3. Pair | C. | Scorch |
| 4. Soothsayer | D. | Darling |
| 5. Step | E. | Also |
| 6. Quote | F. | Perused |

## Language Teaser 28

 Difficulty: medium

The moral of the following story can be expressed by replacing some of the words from a common phrase with rhyming words. For example, a story about a group of amphibians that pool their money together and take over the world might have the moral "Every frog has its pay," derived from the phrase "Every dog has its day." Can you determine the moral to this story?

The woman was hosting a dinner party later in the evening. It was about noon, and she decided to take a nap before preparing the food for the party. Unfortunately, she overslept and had no food ready for her guests. The moral of this story is _____.

## Language Teaser 29

 Difficulty: hard

The clues will lead you to two words that are anagrams of each other. (That is, both words contain the same letters, just in a different order.) For example, the clue "Attach father" would lead you to the anagram "Add Dad."

1. Not above the arm joint
2. Tutors a mutant creature
3. Swindler of a large area of land
4. Mountainous friends
5. Directional soup

## Language Teaser 30

⚠ Difficulty: hard

Here are some more anagram puzzles. The clues will lead you to two words that are anagrams of each other.

1. Swallow stopper
2. Puzzle devourers
3. Unsolicited mail about an atlas
4. Rent painter stand
5. Ruffians with fragrant, pinkish flowers

## *Fact*

An *anagram* is a rearrangement of the letters of a word or phrase to form a different word or phrase. For example, "stable" is an anagram of "bleats" because it uses the same letters in a different order.

# Chapter 4
# Letter Equation Teasers

L etter equations are well-known phrases or facts that have been disguised by replacing key words with the first letter of each word. For example, 12 = I in a F is the letter equation for "12 inches in a foot." Your job is to work out the original fact or phrase.

### Letter Equation Teaser 1

⚠ Difficulty: easy

$12 = M$ in a $Y$

### Letter Equation Teaser 2

⚠ Difficulty: medium

$6 = P$ on a $PT$

### Letter Equation Teaser 3

⚠ Difficulty: hard

$12 = M$ on the $M$

### Letter Equation Teaser 4

⚠ Difficulty: easy

$1 = P$ of $P$ $P$ that $P$ $P$ $P$

## *Essential*

When you see a letter equation, take a look at the number before you start trying to work out what the letters represent. See if you can think of any reasons that the number might be important. Sometimes you can get the solution without even looking at the letters.

## Letter Equation Teaser 5

⚠ Difficulty: medium

13 = C in a S

## Letter Equation Teaser 6

⚠ Difficulty: hard

21 = D on a D

## Letter Equation Teaser 7

⚠ Difficulty: hard

24 = L in the G A

## Letter Equation Teaser 8

⚠ Difficulty: easy

1,000 = W a P is W

## Letter Equation Teaser 9

⚠ Difficulty: easy

26.2 = M in a M

## Letter Equation Teaser 10

⚠ Difficulty: medium

5 = R on the O F

## Letter Equation Teaser 11

⚠ Difficulty: easy

99 = B of B on the W

## Letter Equation Teaser 12

⚠ Difficulty: hard

5 = S on the C F

## Letter Equation Teaser 13

⚠ Difficulty: medium

100 = Z in a G

## Letter Equation Teaser 14

⚠ Difficulty: easy

60 = MPH that a C can R

## Letter Equation Teaser 15

⚠ Difficulty: easy

9 = P on a B F

## Letter Equation Teaser 16

⚠ Difficulty: medium

2 = T D and a P in a P T

## Letter Equation Teaser 17

⚠ Difficulty: medium

88 = K on a P

## Letter Equation Teaser 18

⚠ Difficulty: hard

2 = S on a T B

## Letter Equation Teaser 19

⚠ Difficulty: medium

3 = L K that L T M

## Letter Equation Teaser 20

⚠ Difficulty: easy

20 = F and T on the H B

## *Fact*

Remember your algebra equations from maths lessons?
For example, A = 15B +C. Well, this is where these teasers
got their start. One of the first letter-equation teasers of
all time was probably 4 = S on a S, which is 4 = Sides on
a Square.

### Letter Equation Teaser 21

⚠ Difficulty: hard

1 C L Y = 354 D

### Letter Equation Teaser 22

⚠ Difficulty: easy

9 = S in T T T

## *Fact*

Once you've gotten the hang of solving letter equations, why not try to make up some of your own? Then you can use them to strain your friends' brains!

### Letter Equation Teaser 23

⚠ Difficulty: medium

10 = E in a D

### Letter Equation Teaser 24

⚠ Difficulty: hard

3 = P C in the C W

## Letter Equation Teaser 25

⚠ Difficulty: easy

$100 = D$ in a M

## Letter Equation Teaser 26

⚠ Difficulty: hard

$23 = P$ of C in the H B

## Letter Equation Teaser 27

⚠ Difficulty: medium

$384,400\ K =$ the D to the M from the E

## Letter Equation Teaser 28

⚠ Difficulty: easy

$2 = L$ in a P of P

## Letter Equation Teaser 29

⚠ Difficulty: easy

$4 = Q$ in a W

# Chapter 5
# Logic Teasers

These types of puzzles require you to use logical reasoning to determine the answer. This means that you will probably have to work through several steps of reasoning to solve them. Some paper and a pencil might help you keep track of the facts. Don't let yourself be misled by red herrings!

## Logic Teaser 1

⚠ Difficulty: hard

Since the turn of the last century, the canal has provided one of the quickest ways to travel from one end of the legendary land of Puzzleonia to the other. Every day, the Sinc or Schwim cruise company provides cruises for passengers to travel the length of the canal.

On one particular cruise, six passengers all required specific conditions during the three-day cruise. The six cabins available are numbered 1 to 6 in succession, and all are on the same floor. The walls of the cabins are extremely thin. These six cabins must be allotted to the passengers according to the following set of instructions.

1. Miss Fortune's work as a travelling salesperson requires that she must use the phone regularly during the journey.
2. Miss D. Werk's lucky number is 5, and she insists on having Cabin 5.
3. Mr. Buss and Mr. Allot often talk to each other during their work as second-hand clock repairmen, and they have a preference for adjacent cabins.
4. Mr. Lastrain, Mr. Buss, and Mr. Meaner are all smokers. Miss D. Werk is affected by smoke and insists upon non-smokers adjacent to her cabin.
5. Mr. Meaner requires silence to work during his travels.

Can you determine how the cabins were allotted?

## Logic Teaser 2

⚠ Difficulty: medium

Bobby Braingle has a bit of a dilemma on his hands. He has accidentally locked his puzzle collection in a combination safe. Being rather dim and absent-minded, he has gone and forgotten the combination.

This safe uses letters instead of numbers. The six letters used in the combination are Z, Y, X, W, V, F. No letter is repeated. Here are three incorrect guesses Bobby has already made:

X Y Z W F V
Z V W X Y F
V W F Z X Y

- In the first guess, only one letter is in its correct place.
- In the second guess, only two letters are in their correct places.
- In the third guess, only three letters are in their correct places.
- Each of the six letters is in its correct place once.

What is the correct combination needed to rescue the puzzle collection?

## Logic Teaser 3

 Difficulty: medium

Bobby Braingle has been shipwrecked, and he is the ship-wreck's lone survivor. Stranded on a rocky desert island, dreaming of doughnuts and dying of thirst, Bobby has luckily found a little stream of water on the shore that has pooled in a crevice. Unfortunately, the only thing he has salvaged from the ship is a spoon. It's of little use in scooping out the water, since the crevice is too narrow and the water level is too low. How does Bobby manage to spoon the water out?

## Logic Teaser 4

 Difficulty: easy

One evening, Bobby Braingle sits at home waiting for his favourite television show to come on. As he glances at the clock face (analogue, with numerals 1 to 12 correctly positioned), Bobby makes an observation. If he were to draw a straight line in the right place, the clock face would be divided in such a way that the sum of the numbers on one side of the line would equal the sum of the numbers on the other side of the line.

Where could Bobby draw the line, and what is the total of the numbers on either side?

## Logic Teaser 5

 Difficulty: easy

Bobby either always lies or always tells the truth. Regardless of which it is, there is one statement that Bobby can never make. What is it?

## *Question?*

**How can I brush up on some logic or maths skills?**
If you can't quite remember which end of an equation is up, there are hundreds of Internet sites that can help you out. For example, check out *en.wikibooks.org* for a refresher. This Web site has dozens of free online textbooks on a variety of topics.

## Logic Teaser 6

 Difficulty: medium

My entire family lives on Neuron Street, and for some strange reason I got to choose where everyone lives.

My mother Vera lives at 2005 Neuron Street.
My cousin Lucy lives at 1150 Neuron Street.
What address does that give me?

## Logic Teaser 7

 Difficulty: medium

Below is a short, three-question quiz about Bobby Braingle. There is a single answer that is comprehensively correct for each question. Can you get them all?

1. The outline of Bobby's family crest is in the shape of a:
   a. Square
   b. Parallelogram
   c. Quadrilateral
   d. Rectangle

2. Bobby's favourite number is:
   a. 5
   b. 12
   c. 7
   d. One of the above
   e. None of the above
   f. 6

3. Bobby's street number is:
   a. 25
   b. Greater than 6
   c. Greater than 9
   d. 7

## Logic Teaser 8

 Difficulty: hard

Some very clever aliens have captured you. As a test of your intelligence, they have poisoned you and placed the antidote in one of two vials, with the second vial containing more of the same poison. They won't tell you which is which. Instead, Vial A has a label that reads, "The label on the other vial is true, and this is the antidote." Vial B has a label that reads, "The label on the other vial is false, but it contains the antidote." Which vial should you drink?

## Logic Teaser 9

 Difficulty: easy

You have four pieces of chain. Each piece is made of three links. What is the smallest number of cuts and mends you need to make to produce a circular chain with all 12 links?

## Logic Teaser 10

 Difficulty: easy

At the annual Puzzleonia Tennis Tournament, 128 players compete in a system where the winner of each round goes on to play another winner until there is a champion. How many games are played in the entire tournament?

### Logic Teaser 11

 Difficulty: medium

The king of Puzzleonia is at a fund-raiser, and he must personally shake hands with all 99 guests – a lot of handshaking. How many handshakes would be made if all 100 people at the fundraiser shook hands with every other person once?

## Fact

Sometimes it is helpful to make a chart listing all possibilities. Then cross off all the possibilities that cannot be true, according to the clues in the logic teaser. This may help you work out the answer.

### Logic Teaser 12

 Difficulty: hard

What is the fewest number of colours you can use to colour in a map of the United States without using the same colour on any adjoining states?

### Logic Teaser 13

 Difficulty: easy

If a dozen chickens can lay 24 eggs in four days, how long does it take one chicken to lay three eggs?

## Logic Teaser 14

 Difficulty: medium

Potato Pete is getting ready to ship a bunch of barrels of potatoes to the local French fry factory. He knows that the French fry factory only buys potatoes that weigh exactly one pound, so he has sorted all the 1-pound potatoes into barrels. He also sorts the potatoes that weight exactly 1.1 pounds into other barrels that he sends to the potato chip factory. Any potatoes that do not weigh 1 or 1.1 pounds are sent to the mashed potato plant.

The problem is that Pete has accidentally swapped one barrel from the potato-chip order with a barrel from the French fry order – and he doesn't know which barrel it is. Luckily, Pete has a scale that will read the weight to three decimal places. What is the smallest number of weighings Pete can make to correct his mistake? You should know that each order has exactly 10 barrels and that no two barrels have the same number of potatoes inside.

## Logic Teaser 15

 Difficulty: medium

A chessboard has eight rows and eight columns. In chess, a rook can move any number of squares at a time, either sideways or forward, but it cannot move diagonally. What is the smallest possible number of moves the rook would have to make to pass over every single square on the board and finish in the same position where it began? The rook can start anywhere.

## Logic Teaser 16

 Difficulty: medium

Adam, Chris, Maggie, and Jeff entered a burping competition. Can you determine their last names, their position in the competition, and what type of drink they drank before their burp?

The last names are Boyle, Burch, Coriano, and Finn. The possible drinks are soda, milk, water, and apple juice.

Clues:
1. Adam Finn beat Maggie by two places.
2. Chris's water-based burp beat Mrs. Burch's son, who came in third.
3. The apple-juice burp, despite being a bit short, made it to the top three because it was so loud.
4. The judges gave second place to the soda burp.
5. Boyle's mother cried as she watched her son take first prize.

## Logic Teaser 17

 Difficulty: medium

Here is a 10-digit number in which the numerals have been replaced with different letters. Each letter always represents the same numeral. From the clues, can you work out what the 10-digit number is?

ABCDDDCDDD

1. A is the number of zeros in the full number.
2. B is the number of ones in the full number.
3. C is the number of twos in the full number.
4. D is the number of threes in the full number.

## Logic Teaser 18

 Difficulty: easy

You just moved into a new flat, and you are about to post your first month's rent. You walk down the hallway and notice that there are three different mail chutes. A sign above reads, "Only one of these is actually a mail chute. The other two go to the skip in the back alley." Naturally, you don't want to send your rent cheque to the skip. How can you determine the correct chute with a minimum of trips up and down the stairs?

## Logic Teaser 19

 Difficulty: easy

A train comes to a bridge that can carry a maximum weight limit of 12 tons. The engine of the train weighs 1 ton, and the four carriages that the train is hauling weigh 11 tons, 7 tons, 5 tons, and 2 tons. The heavier the load, the slower the train is able to travel. It takes the engine one minute to cross the bridge for every ton of weight that it is pulling, including itself. (For example, if the 1-ton engine were hauling an 8-ton carriage, it would take nine minutes to cross the bridge.)

What is the least amount of time required for the entire train to cross the bridge? Assume that it doesn't take any time to hook and unhook carriages at both ends and that there is a turntable at each end to move the carriages around in any order.

## Logic Teaser 20

 Difficulty: easy

Six cars finished a race. The red car finished before the blue car but after the green car. The yellow car finished before the black car but behind the blue car. The white car finished exactly one car before the yellow car. In which order did the cars finish?

## Logic Teaser 21

 Difficulty: medium

Five customers (Candy, Derek, John, Rose, and Steve), order lunch at a fast-food restaurant. They order the following things, not in order: cheeseburger, salad, chicken nuggets, hamburger, and fried fish. Each customer asks for his or her meal with extra sauce (ketchup, mustard, barbeque sauce, mayo, and chilli sauce). Can you work out who got what and in which order they were standing in line?

Clues:

1. The first customer (who wasn't a girl) isn't the one who ordered a salad.
2. The salad did not have barbeque sauce on it.
3. Candy ate chicken for lunch and wasn't last in line.
4. The person who asked for extra ketchup had a cheeseburger.
5. John did not eat the mustard-drenched fish.
6. Derek was in the exact middle of the line.
7. Steve was in line after the salad-eater but before the mayo-lover.

## Logic Teaser 22

 Difficulty: medium

Bobby Braingle is shopping at the grocery store. He purchases some apples, oranges, bananas, nectarines, and pineapples. Each fruit cost £1, £2, £3, £4, or £5 apiece, and Bobby purchased either one, two, three, four, or five pieces of each fruit. Can you work out exactly what Bobby purchased?

Clues:

1. The £2 orange was delicious.
2. Bobby bought more apples than oranges, but fewer apples than the £4 fruit.
3. Bobby spent £20 total on peaches.
4. The two £5 fruits needed to be peeled.
5. He did not purchase four apples or four nectarines.
6. The pineapples cost £10, which was more than Bobby spent on bananas.

## Logic Teaser 23

 Difficulty: easy

Sue, Tina, and Shannon are the treasurer, historian, and president of their local book club, although not in that order. At the last meeting, the treasurer, an only child, spoke the least. Shannon, who is married to Sue's brother, spoke more than the historian. Who does what?

## Logic Teaser 24

 Difficulty: medium

Three aliens are on the alien basketball team. Each alien has a different number of limbs (either two, three, or four). Each alien is wearing a jersey with a number printed on it. Coincidentally, the numbers are 2, 3, and 4. The alien wearing the number 4 jersey says, "Isn't it odd that our jersey numbers match the number of our limbs, but none of us is actually wearing the jersey number that matches our own number of limbs?" The three-limbed alien turns around and says, "Yeah, that is strange."

Which alien is wearing which jersey number?

## *Fact*

Sometimes a logic teaser seems to contain a paradox, or a statement that is self-contradictory or contrary to the other established facts. A variant on a famous ancient Greek paradox is the statement, "I am a Texan, and I know that everyone from Texas is a constant liar." When you think you see a paradox, pay attention, as this could be the point the puzzle hinges on.

## Logic Teaser 25

 Difficulty: easy

Grandma has five apples and five grandchildren. She wants to feed all of her grandchildren an equal amount of apple, but the apples are all different sizes, so she can't work out how to give each grandchild an equal amount. Can you help her?

## Logic Teaser 26

 Difficulty: hard

Five friends (Bobby, Isaac, Isabel, Mimi, and Shane) are playing a baseball game against some other people. Each friend plays a different position (first base, pitcher, shortstop, catcher, right field) and makes a different number of hits (one, two, three, four, or five). From the clues can you work out who did what?

Clues:

1. Bobby, the furthest from home base, had exactly twice as many hits as the pitcher.
2. The shortstop was tired after getting her fifth hit.
3. Shane had more hits than all the other infielders except for Isabel.
4. Isaac wears a mask.

## Logic Teaser 27

 Difficulty: easy

Next week I want to go into town and have lunch with my brother, borrow a book at the library, meet a colleague, and get my hair cut. My brother is busy on Wednesday. My colleague has a weekend trip planned. The library is closed for cleaning on Tuesday and Thursday, and it isn't open on the weekends. My hair stylist only has appointments free on Tuesday, Friday, and Saturday. How can I make the fewest trips into town?

## Chapter 6
# Maths Teasers

All of these teasers require you to do some sort of calculation to arrive at the answer. Some knowledge of geometry or trigonometry may be needed for some of these puzzles, but don't fret. Usually a little drawing and some common sense will be enough to get the job done.

## Maths Teaser 1

 Difficulty: hard

Predictably, Bobby Braingle is once again waiting for the Puzzle Shop to open (he always gets there early). This time, he has arrived over an hour early, and as a consequence stands looking at his watch and counting the seconds and minutes until the shop opens. He noticed something strange about his watch: The minute and the hour hands of his watch meet exactly every 65 minutes. How much time would Bobby's watch gain or lose in an hour, if any?

## Maths Teaser 2

 Difficulty: medium

Long ago, the king of Puzzleonia lost the combination to the safe where the secret biscuit recipe is held. He sent for Al Krakit, the most prolific safe-cracker in the prison system, and offered him a royal pardon if he succeeded in opening the safe.

After several attempts at bypassing the combination, Al Krakit has realized that the only way to open the safe safely is to try every possible combination by hand. The special lock has a four-character code. Two of the characters must be letters, and the lock is case sensitive (with AB not the same as ab). The other two must be digits, anything from 0 to 9.

What is the maximum number of combinations that Al Krakit would have to try before finding the correct code?

## Maths Teaser 3

 Difficulty: medium

In the general meeting of Puzzleonia's Secret Society of Athletes, Chairman Bobby Braingle said, "The repairs to the club after the last all-night wrestling match will come to a total of £3,120. I propose that this amount should be met by the members, each paying an equal amount." The proposal was immediately agreed upon, more out of embarrassment than anything else. However, four members of the society chose to resign, leaving the remaining members to pay an extra £26 each.

How many members did the secret society originally have?

## Maths Teaser 4

 Difficulty: hard

Bobby Braingle is at his local news-stand, looking at the various magazines on display. He picked up a copy of *Pretzels and Me,* a copy of *Wooden Puzzles Digest,* and a copy of *Indoor Hang Gliding.* He passes the magazines to the shopkeeper, who enters the amounts of each magazine into the cash register.

"Hang on a minute!" says Bobby. "You just pressed the multiplication button each time between amounts instead of the addition button." The shopkeeper smiles with new false teeth and replies, "It doesn't matter. Either way, it comes to £5.70."

What were the prices of the magazines?

## Maths Teaser 5

 Difficulty: easy

Wally Rus and Rod Lightning decide to race each other to the Puzzle Shop, exactly one mile away, and then back again. Wally, being on the chubby side, runs at 10 mph to the shop, but he manages a whopping 30 mph on the way back (downhill with a tail wind). Rod Lightning, on the other hand, being less weight-challenged than Wally, runs at a constant rate of 20 mph each way.

Who wins the race?

## Maths Teaser 6

 Difficulty: medium

There has been a shipwreck, and Bobby Braingle, Smelly Pickels, and an Elvis impersonator named Elmer McPresley are washed ashore on a small island. Reaching the shore, exhausted, they all fall asleep. Bobby awakes first and sees that a box of doughnuts has been washed ashore. Greedy as he is, he eats a third of the doughnuts and goes back to sleep. Next Smelly wakes up. Seeing the box of doughnuts, he eats a third of what is left and goes back to sleep. Elmer wakes up next. Assuming that the other two haven't eaten any doughnuts, he eats a third of what remains. When Elmer has finished, there are eight doughnuts left.

How many doughnuts were in the box originally?

## Maths Teaser 7

 Difficulty: easy

In Puzzleonia, every horse is required to be licensed. A horse licence-number is made up of one letter and one digit. What is the maximum number of horses that can be licensed in Puzzleonia under this system?

## Maths Teaser 8

 Difficulty: easy

Bobby Braingle and Hyde Enceek are on a backpacking trip. Bobby carried the heavy backpack for the first 4 miles, and Hyde carried it the rest of the way into the campsite. The next morning they fished a bit and packed up to return home along the same path they had used yesterday. This time Bobby started again with the heavy backpack, and Hyde finished off by carrying it out the last 5 miles. Who carried the backpack the most and by how much?

## *Alert!*

Before you try to solve a mathematical teaser, be sure you understand what information you have and what information you need to solve the problem. Sometimes the information you need can be calculated as a side problem. If you can break the problem into two smaller pieces, it will be easier to solve them independently.

## Maths Teaser 9

 Difficulty: medium

As the newest faculty member of the Advanced Materials Department of the College of Puzzleonia, you are in charge of examining new materials and sending them along to the appropriate department. One day you receive a piece of cloth exactly 10 cm by 10 cm square. You are told that it is a special fabric that cannot be cut or torn. You immediately recognize that this cloth belongs in the textiles department so you prepare to send it by inter-office robot courier. For some silly reason the robot can only accept square envelopes with an area of exactly 50 cm. How can you fold the cloth so that it fits into the appropriate envelope?

## Maths Teaser 10

 Difficulty: easy

Bobby Braingle works at the Freshest Doughnut Store. The doughnut machine normally produces one fresh doughnut every 18 seconds, but it broke some time ago. The last nine doughnuts produced are still sitting on the tray. The oldest doughnut is five times older than the freshest doughnut. Bobby is trying to work out how long ago the machine broke. What is the shortest amount of time it could have been broken?

## Maths Teaser 11

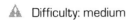 Difficulty: medium

You enter a strange contest in which you pay one penny to start a clock. The clock always starts at noon, and once it starts, your money will begin doubling every minute. You can stop the clock whenever you want and take your money out. However, you can only keep your money if the digits of your total include two consecutive 8s and the total is less than $1 million. At what time should you stop the clock?

## Maths Teaser 12

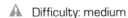 Difficulty: medium

If you take all the prime numbers under 1,000,000 and multiply them together, what digit will be in the one's place?

## Maths Teaser 13

 Difficulty: easy

A monk has a very specific ritual for climbing up the steps to the temple, which for religious reasons are odd in number. First he climbs up to the middle step and meditates for one minute. Then he climbs up eight steps and faces east until he hears a bird singing. Then he walks down 12 steps and picks up a pebble. He takes one step up and tosses the pebble over his left shoulder. Now, he walks up the remaining steps two at a time, which only takes him 14 paces. How many steps are there at the temple?

## Maths Teaser 14

 Difficulty: hard

Several contestants were in a chocolate-bunny-eating contest. After the contestants stuffed their faces for 20 minutes, all of the bunnies were eaten. One of the contestants remarked, "Isn't it interesting that there were seven times as many bunnies as contestants, but that each of us ate a different number of bunnies?" Another contestant replies, "That certainly is interesting. I always eat the ears first, and I noticed that when we had eaten a third of the bunnies, there were four fewer than 10 times as many bunny ears as human noses in the contest."

How many bunnies and contestants were in the contest?

## Maths Teaser 15

 Difficulty: medium

A baby squirrel can dig an acorn hole in 10 seconds. A mummy squirrel can dig an acorn hole in 5 seconds, and a daddy squirrel can dig an acorn hole in 2.5 seconds. If the entire family works together, how quickly can they dig one acorn hole?

## Maths Teaser 16

 Difficulty: hard

Bobby Braingle has just been given a new watch by his wife. He looks at the watch and sees that it is already set to the correct time of 8:00 p.m. Over the next few hours, he notices that his new watch is losing six minutes per hour. When will his watch again read the correct time?

## Maths Teaser 17

 Difficulty: easy

I just bought £1,024 worth of concert tickets for my gardening club. We're going to go see the Roots Down Under next week at the concert hall. Each ticket was the same price, and interestingly, the cost of an individual ticket is exactly the number of tickets that I bought. How many did I buy?

## Maths Teaser 18

 Difficulty: medium

You have a bag of pennies, and you are arranging them on the table. You notice that you can make a solid triangle with six pennies and a solid square with nine pennies. What is the smallest number of pennies that you can use, with none left over, that can be used to make either a triangle or a square?

### Maths Teaser 19

 Difficulty: hard

What nine-digit number is divisible by 11 and has no repeating digits?

### Maths Teaser 20

 Difficulty: easy

You have two very hungry termites and two sticks of wood. One stick of wood is 12 inches long, and the other is 16 inches long. One termite can eat wood at the rate of 1 inch every three minutes. The slower termite can eat 1 inch of wood in four minutes. How would you use both of the termites and wooden sticks to measure 48 minutes?

## *Essential*

Are you stumped? Make a drawing. Sometimes drawing a little graph or making a chart will help you put the problem in perspective. If you can draw the problem, you'll be one step closer to solving it.

### Maths Teaser 21

 Difficulty: medium

Using the same termites and the same wooden sticks, how would you measure 61 minutes?

## Maths Teaser 22

 Difficulty: medium

Bobby Braingle just got one of those new hybrid automobiles that uses very little fuel. He tests out the car on his drive to work. To get to work, Bobby must drive 10 miles uphill and 5 miles on flat land; to get home, it's 5 miles flat, and 10 miles downhill. After several weeks of testing, he determines that his new car gets 35 miles per gallon (mpg) going uphill, 80 mpg downhill, and 50 mpg on level terrain. What is the average mileage Bobby gets on his complete round trip?

## Maths Teaser 23

 Difficulty: easy

A perfect square is made by multiplying a number by itself. A perfect cube is made by multiplying a number by itself twice. What two-digit number sits exactly between a perfect square and a perfect cube?

## Maths Teaser 24

 Difficulty: hard

In my entire life, I have blown out 528 birthday candles. How old am I? (See if you can do it without adding them all up.)

## Maths Teaser 25

 Difficulty: medium

A 10-foot rope is tied from a hook on the ceiling to a hook on the floor. There is no slack in the rope. Bobby Braingle wants to tie up his dog so he can go and do a little shopping. He detaches the rope from the hook on the floor and attaches the free end to the dog's collar, which happens to be 2 feet off the floor. (It's a big dog.) The dog can now run around in a circle, and because the rope goes to the ceiling the dog won't trip or get tangled up in the rope. What a good idea! What is the radius of the circle in which the dog can wander?

## Maths Teaser 26

 Difficulty: hard

Santa Claus sometimes helps the elves make toys. He's not as fast as they are, but he can still make 30 toys each hour. In order to keep from getting bored he starts each day by building 50 trains and then switches to building 50 airplanes. Then he switches back to trains and keeps switching back and forth doing 50 of each until the day is finished. If Santa starts work at 8:00 A.M., when will he finish his 108th train?

## Maths Teaser 27

 Difficulty: easy

Tom, Karin, and Sherri decide to see who can do the most pushups. Together, Tom and Karin complete 43 press-ups. The sum of Karin and Sherri's press-ups is 41. If you add Sherri's pushups to Tom's, you will have 38. Who did the most press-ups?

## Maths Teaser 28

 Difficulty: medium

In a five-day working week, Bobby Braingle manufactures 1,000 pogo sticks at the factory. Each day he builds 30 more sticks than the day before. How many pogo sticks did Bobby build on Monday?

## Maths Teaser 29

 Difficulty: easy

What is half of four plus four?

## Chapter 7
# Probability Teasers

All of the puzzles in this section involve probability. To solve some of these puzzles you need to weigh the possibilities of different outcomes according to the information given. Others require you to work out the probability of multiple events happening in order.

## Probability Teaser 1

⚠ Difficulty: easy

Consider a simple weekly lottery. A number between 1 and 1,000,000 (inclusive) is randomly chosen each week. What are your odds of winning in each of the following?

1. If you play one number this week, what are your odds of winning?
2. If you win this week, what are your odds of winning by choosing the same number next week?
3. If you win this week, what are your odds of winning by choosing a different number next week?
4. What are the odds that 50 will be the winning number two weeks in a row?
5. What are the odds that the winning number will be the same two weeks in a row?

## Probability Teaser 2

⚠ Difficulty: medium

Above you is a rope attached to a shower head. You make a bet with your friend. The two of you will take turns standing in the shower and giving the rope a single pull; the first person to get wet has to buy dinner. You know that the shower works properly on three consecutive pulls of the rope. After those three pulls, it takes another three to reset the shower, during which the shower stays dry. You don't know where the shower is in its cycle. Should you go first or second?

## Probability Teaser 3

 Difficulty: medium

Bobby Braingle has a fatal disease, but he has no money or insurance to pay for the cure. The only thing he can do is sign up for an experimental medical and psychological test. The doctor brings him two jars of pills, identical except for their colour. One jar contains 50 red pills, and the other contains 50 blue pills. The doctor says that the red pills are nothing but placebos (sugar pills), while the blue pills contain a cure for his illness. Bobby is supposed to mix the pills in any way that he wants between the two jars. Blindfolded, he will then have to pick a single pill from a single jar, at random. How should he mix the pills to ensure the highest chance of survival?

## Probability Teaser 4

 Difficulty: easy

You have a box that contains 11 baby ducks and 17 baby chicks. You also have a number of baby chicks running around on the floor. You decide to play a little game. You will remove two birds at random from the box. If the birds are the same, you will place them onto the floor, and then pick up a chick and put it into the box. If they are different, you will put the duck back and place the chick on the floor. What is the last bird remaining in the box, a chick or a duck?

### Probability Teaser 5

 Difficulty: hard

A line of 200 people waits to get in to a theatre with 200 seats. Each person has an assigned seat – except for the first person in line, who is a VIP and will sit anywhere he wants. Any person with an assigned seat who finds that his or her seat is occupied will pick another seat at random. What is the likelihood that the last person in line will sit in his or her assigned seat?

## *Essential*

> Here's a tip for solving probability teasers. If you have two independent events, and the probabilities of them happening are A and B, the probability of both of them happening is A times B (A × B). The probability of either of them happening is A plus B (A + B).

### Probability Teaser 6

 Difficulty: easy

You have two coins. One is normal, and the other is a trick coin with two heads. You have both of them in your pocket. If you reach into your pocket, remove one coin and the side you look at happens to be a head, what is the probability that the other side is also a head?

## Probability Teaser 7

 Difficulty: hard

You are at a party with 11 other people. The announcer asks everyone to pick a number between 1 and 100. What are the odds that each person selected a different number?

## Probability Teaser 8

 Difficulty: medium

Bobby Braingle closes his eyes and tosses a draughts piece onto a draughtboard. The draughtboard measures 12 inches on a side. There are eight squares to a side, and the draughts piece measures 1 inch in diameter. What is the probability that the draughts piece is not touching a line?

## Probability Teaser 9

 Difficulty: easy

Bobby really likes doughnuts. His two favourite doughnut shops are at the North End and South End stations of the underground. Every morning Bobby takes a walk to the underground station near his house, which happens to be in the exact centre of the underground line. Because Bobby is always in a hurry to eat doughnuts, he always takes the first train that he sees. Interestingly, he ends up visiting the South End shop four times as often as the North End shop. What is a possible underground timetable?

## Probability Teaser 10

⚠ Difficulty: medium

A woman has two children. At least one of them is a boy. What is the probability that the other child is also a boy?

## Probability Teaser 11

⚠ Difficulty: easy

A big game of Simon Says has 100 contestants. Each person will mess up once every 25 rounds. What are the odds that Contestant 60 will win?

## Probability Teaser 12

⚠ Difficulty: medium

If you take a random glance at your watch, what are the odds that the time will contain consecutive digits, such as 1:23?

## Probability Teaser 13

⚠ Difficulty: easy

Bobby and Nobby are shooting free throws on the basketball court. Bobby shoots 60 times, and Nobby shoots 40 times. Each makes 20 baskets. The next day Bobby makes 10 baskets out of 60 attempts. Nobby is tired. He only shoots 40 times and doesn't make any baskets. Who has a better percentage over the two days?

## Probability Teaser 14

 Difficulty: medium

On a visit to the US I play a game in a bar. I have three cups facedown on the table in front of me. Under each cup is a coin, either a nickel, a dime, or a quarter. Now I'm going to mix up the cups and let you choose one. You can either keep the coin underneath or choose the coin from another cup. We'll play this game several times. Clearly you will keep the quarter if you pick it, and switch the nickel. What should you do if you pick the dime?

## *Fact*

Did you know that when you toss a coin, the probability of its landing on heads is not 50 percent? Because a coin is essentially a very short cylinder, there is a slight chance that the coin could land on its edge and thus be neither heads nor tails.

## Probability Teaser 15

 Difficulty: hard

A frog sits on a log in a hole in the bottom of the sea. Each of his four feet has four toes. Each toe has two warts. This species of frog can have red, blue, or purple warts. What is the probability that this particular frog has all purple warts?

## Probability Teaser 16

Difficulty: medium

A family has signed up to play a game of wits. The family has nine members lined up shoulder to shoulder. Each person chooses whether to hold a red or blue marble. The caller randomly selects a family member to reveal his or her marble. If the marble is blue, that person must wear a dunce's cap. If the marble is red, the round is over and all players reveal their marbles. At this point, everyone standing directly to the left of a red-marble-holder must wear a dunce's cap. If the family has five or more members left without caps, then they win. To maximize the chances of success, who should be holding red marbles and who blue?

## Probability Teaser 17

Difficulty: hard

In Puzzleonia, 7 percent of the people are chronic liars. A lie detector test is only 95-percent accurate. A random person is asked a simple question under the lie detector and test results are positive; that is, they show that the person is a liar. What is the probability that the person really is a liar?

## Probability Teaser 18

 Difficulty: easy

Bobby Braingle is sorting plants at the nursery. He accidentally mixes up the labels on four of the plants (tomato, courgettes, peppers, and green beans). What is the probability that exactly three of the plants will grow up to be what they were marked?

## Probability Teaser 19

 Difficulty: hard

The Kiddie Meal at the local fast-food restaurant comes with one of three different toys inside. If your child wants to collect all three toys, how many Kiddie Meals should she expect to eat on average?

## Probability Teaser 20

 Difficulty: easy

Bobby Braingle takes 27 sugar cubes and stacks them into a larger cube with three sugar cubes to a side. He then paints the entire surface of the large cube green, so of the original 162 white faces of the sugar cubes, 54 are now green. If Bobby bumps the table so that the big green cube falls apart, what is the probability that the cubes will fall in such a way that all the face-up surfaces are green?

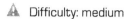
### Probability Teaser 21

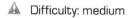 Difficulty: medium

You are playing a unique new game at a casino. You roll one die, and the casino rolls two. If your number is between the two numbers rolled by the casino, then you win. The casino wins any ties. What is your probability of winning?

## *Question?*

**Should I play the lottery?**
The probability of winning the lottery is extremely slim. In fact, if you purchase a ticket today for next week's lottery, you are 10 times more likely to die before the numbers are drawn than you are to win. Do you have life insurance?

### Probability Teaser 22

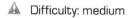 Difficulty: medium

What is the probability that the difference between two randomly chosen single-digit numbers is greater than 5?

## Probability Teaser 23

 Difficulty: medium

Bobby Braingle is taking his family to the cinema. Bobby has a large family of 11 members, and luckily they find an empty row that has exactly 11 seats. Bobby makes a rule that after the first person sits down, the next person and all subsequent people to sit down must take a seat adjacent to another family member. How many possible ways can the family sit down?

## Probability Teaser 24

 Difficulty: easy

Bobby Braingle is the owner of a brand-new hotel. He has 500 rooms numbered 101 to 600. What is the probability that a randomly placed guest will have a room number that starts with 1, 2, or 3 and that ends with 4, 5, or 6?

## Probability Teaser 25

 Difficulty: hard

There is a birthday party with both girl and boy guests. Someone ate the last piece of cake, but the details are a bit sketchy. Let's assume that statistically, the last piece of cake is eaten by a boy 85 percent of the time. The adult in charge thought that she saw a girl eat the last piece, but we know that the adult is only correct 80 percent of the time. What is the probability that a girl ate the last piece of cake? What is the probability that it was a boy?

## Probability Teaser 26

⚠ Difficulty: medium

In Puzzleonia, boys are born more frequently than girls. Boys make up 52 percent of all births, and girls make up the other 48 percent. What is the probability that a family of four children will have exactly two boys and two girls?

## Probability Teaser 27

⚠ Difficulty: easy

I have a CD with 10 tracks on it. I like to play it with my stereo set on shuffle. The way my stereo works is that it will play all 10 songs in a random order without repeating any of them. Then, if I let it keep going, my stereo will play all 10 songs again in a different random order. Using this method, it is possible that my stereo could play the same song twice in a row. What is that probability?

## Chapter 8
# Rebus Teasers

These types of teasers use words or letters in unusual configurations to represent common phrases or facts. You must decode the phrase or fact by deciphering the placement clues.

### Rebus Teaser 1

 Difficulty: easy

STRUmusicalMENTS

### Rebus Teaser 2

 Difficulty: easy

YOU JUST ME

### Rebus Teaser 3

 Difficulty: medium

Beatles
*Titanic*

W
E
'R
E

### Rebus Teaser 4

 Difficulty: hard

+´

### Rebus Teaser 5

 Difficulty: medium

GRH2OAH2OVE

## Rebus Teaser 6

 Difficulty: hard

HICANS

## Rebus Teaser 7

Difficulty: easy

ECNALG

## Rebus Teaser 8

Difficulty: hard

EAREAR

## Rebus Teaser 9

Difficulty: hard

O_ER_T_O_

## Rebus Teaser 10

Difficulty: medium

ENTURY

## Rebus Teaser 11

 Difficulty: easy

STEP PETS PETS

## Rebus Teaser 12

▲ Difficulty: medium

cHIMp

## Rebus Teaser 13

▲ Difficulty: easy

IGAR
CIGR
CGAR
CIGA
CIAR

## Rebus Teaser 14

▲ Difficulty: easy

NOSE
SSSS
CHIN

## Rebus Teaser 15

▲ Difficulty: easy

| T | M | C |
|---|---|---|
| A | U | O |
| H | S | M |
| W | T | E |

### Rebus Teaser 16

 Difficulty: medium

eyee cexcept

### Rebus Teaser 17

 Difficulty: easy

Close Close
Comfort Comfort Comfort Comfort

### Rebus Teaser 18

 Difficulty: easy

eeee
e
eee
e
eeee

pppp
p
ppp
p
pppp

### Rebus Teaser 19

 Difficulty: medium

Guyyyy

### Rebus Teaser 20

⚠ Difficulty: hard

SEcu4rE

### Rebus Teaser 21

⚠ Difficulty: medium

biddenbiddenbiddenbiddenfruit

### Rebus Teaser 22

⚠ Difficulty: easy

smupoke

### Rebus Teaser 23

⚠ Difficulty: medium

getgetitgetget

### Rebus Teaser 24

⚠ Difficulty: medium

KNOWITNO

### Rebus Teaser 25

⚠ Difficulty: medium

Cont_ol

### Rebus Teaser 26

 Difficulty: hard

Off to dinner and a movie
Leg

### Rebus Teaser 27

 Difficulty: easy

NE
RV
OU
S

## *Essential*

A common trick with rebus teasers is to place one word inside or on top of another word to create "on" or "in." For example, "awhONCEile" would be "once IN awhile."

### Rebus Teaser 28

 Difficulty: medium

PICT RES

### Rebus Teaser 29

 Difficulty: easy

sssssssssse

## Chapter 9
# Riddle Teasers

Riddles are little poems or verses that sometimes rhyme and always pose a question that needs answering. Usually the riddle will describe something and you'll need to work out what the mystery thing is.

### Riddle Teaser 1

 Difficulty: hard

A potato's key tool, I have all the power.
I am generally used on the half or full hour.
If my cells were deceased or lost or the such,
Only my partner would respond to your touch.
*What am I?*

### Riddle Teaser 2

 Difficulty: medium

My closest friends are very tense.
I'm difficult to use and hence
I'm beautiful with learned hand.
With untrained folk I'm not so grand.
You know not what I am, you say?
Well, half of me's already given away.
*What am I?*

### Riddle Teaser 3

 Difficulty: easy

We're the measure of hunger and also of power.
Four of us will bring on the final hour.
Some gain wealth on account of our speed.
Once we are broken to man we will heed.
*What are we?*

### Riddle Teaser 4

 Difficulty: medium

Drink like us and you'll need be excused.
Sleep with us and your soul's diffused.
*What are we?*

### Riddle Teaser 5

 Difficulty: medium

I can outrun a horse.
I can roar like a lion.
But unlike my brothers
I can't do no flyin'.
*What am I?*

### Riddle Teaser 6

 Difficulty: medium

To some a bloated ball of gas,
To others I'm a king.
I'll stare you down with one red eye
Or fry you with lightning.
*What am I?*

### Riddle Teaser 7

 Difficulty: hard

Odds are good you know my start
But do not know my end.
I sound delicious but I'm not
Be sure of that, my friend.

A squiggle here, two squiggles there,
Is clearly what you'll see.
From here to there, how far around?
Well, it's all Greek to me.
*What am I?*

### Riddle Teaser 8

 Difficulty: hard

The rodents walk all over me.
Well, "walk" is not the word.
My job is to exist
And not much else, you've heard.

I see the end is nearing, though.
My usefulness, it dies.
Since those clever scientific types
Replaced the balls with eyes.
*What am I?*

## Riddle Teaser 9

 Difficulty: hard

> There was a young woman from Troy
> Who possessed a remarkable toy.
> Ate up sunshine it did
> Except for that which was hid
> And remembered the look of her boy.
>
> There was yet another from Dreck
> Whose toy was much more low-tech.
> With a twist and a turn
> She could draw up an urn
> But up-ended would go straight to heck.
>
> What objects did each woman have?

## Riddle Teaser 10

 Difficulty: medium

> You could say I'm a welcome mat,
> Though "mat" would be untrue.
> I've travelled one great ocean
> But in toppled form – boo hoo!
>
> Those that first observed me
> Would know that I'm changed today.
> First as brown and then to green.
> It's in the air, they say.
> *What am I?*

## Riddle Teaser 11

 Difficulty: easy

> Worth more to its owner than others would pay.
> The undying token of one glorious day.
> It notes the beginning and shows of no end.
> A constant reminder of one true, dear friend.
> *What is it?*

## Riddle Teaser 12

 Difficulty: easy

> I am the mother of you all,
> Although I come real cheap.
> I am often discarded
> Into a shameful heap.
>
> Oft compared to stars above
> (Well, at least in number).
> Just existing, not much else,
> Like an eternal slumber.
>
> 'Tis a shame those you treat bad
> Are said to be like me,
> When I'm of infinite importance –
> Just go ask a tree.
> *What am I?*

## *Alert!*

Don't take riddles too literally. These teasers use metaphors and similes for their artistic effect. You'll need to see through all these layers to work out what the riddle is really about.

## Riddle Teaser 13

 Difficulty: medium

A sneaker I'm not, though much the same
(Just think of what I do).
My only master comes up lame,
If I should be run through.

Left or right, to or fro,
I'll take you anywhere.
I often take a welcome rest
When master's in repair.
*What am I?*

## Riddle Teaser 14

⚠ Difficulty: medium

Seven of us you will find,
Each bigger than the next.
Where to put our members
Often leaves our users vexed.

The first is like a monarch
Without the regal dress.
The third is where you go to learn.
The fourth is not a mess.

The fifth is much like Mom and Dad
And brothers, sisters too.
The sixth a smart man less an "I,"
The last is me and you.

But wait! I left out number two.
Am I dumber than a camel?
If you guess it anyway
I'll admit you're one smart mammal.
*What are these seven things?*

## Riddle Teaser 15

 Difficulty: easy

Five friends are we, all holding hands.
We're known throughout the many lands.
The first are mournful, evil, mad.
Then fearful, jealous (yes, it's sad).

From the land of Zeus we hail,
Laid upon our wintry sail.
The human spirit we denote.
Where we fly is up to vote.

"But stop. That first verse makes no sense."
Ah, you're confused, my friend, and hence,
Instead of rainbows in your head,
Emotions you think of instead.
*What are these five things?*

## Riddle Teaser 16

 Difficulty: easy

Left is right, right is left –
Well, that's not really true.
What you see when you see me
Is what I see of you.
*What am I?*

### Riddle Teaser 17

 Difficulty: easy

> There was a young man from Dunbar
> Whose wife thought she'd be gifted a car.
> But she could store no junk
> In the blasted thing's trunk
> Still, the horn could be heard from afar.
>
> There was a young woman from Durst
> Who got the same gift as the first.
> She really didn't need it
> And nor could she feed it.
> Of all, though, the smell was the worst.
> *What is the gift?*

### Riddle Teaser 18

 Difficulty: hard

> I think I know just when you'll die
> And if you'll make it big.
> My users are extravagant.
> My dimensions are quite trig.
>
> Hanged man, devils, stars, and death
> Are what I've come to show.
> A sceptic are you? Well, we'll see
> How much of you I know.
> *What am I?*

## Riddle Teaser 19

 Difficulty: medium

To some I'm like Bee, to some I'm like Fred.
After me, as you know, the procession is dead.
Very important but often unused,
Beaten out by my friend for a role in "Confused."
*What am I?*

## Riddle Teaser 20

 Difficulty: easy

I cast royalty among the masses
With no concern for rank or classes.
Strewn about in random order
Though tricksters can control my borders.

I am an action, not a thing
Like running, walking, or speaking.
My job, it is part of the game:
To separate what are the same.
*What am I?*

## Riddle Teaser 21

 Difficulty: hard

> Over hills and valleys do I wing,
> Searching for the vilest things.
> And when I find them I will stride
> To cast the vile things aside.
>
> The irony that you must see
> Is that the one who commands me
> Is the one who put them there
> Now he wants them to disappear.
>
> You say there's too much metaphor,
> And that your brain is getting sore?
> Here's one last hint (if not too late),
> The hills are metaphor times eight.
> *What am I?*

## Riddle Teaser 22

 Difficulty: hard

> It's a shame one so supportive
> Should be so much feared.
> Ten score plus a handful
> And another by your beard.
> *What is it?*

## Riddle Teaser 23

 Difficulty: easy

> Four, five, six, then one, then two.
> I think someone can't count, don't you?
> Far-off lands with far-off people.
> A religion with no church or steeple.
>
> All this is from the past, but then,
> Seems futuristic to us men.
> In a universe that is torn
> In '77 it was born.
> *What is this?*

## Riddle Teaser 24

 Difficulty: medium

> 'Tis a shame that those so great
> Would give their lives for me.
> You take the grandest of your kin
> To fill my endless sea.
>
> 'Twas promised that this act would slow
> When chips were brought about.
> But 'tis a sad fact we all know:
> I can't be done without.
> *What am I?*

### Riddle Teaser 25

⚠ Difficulty: hard

There was a man from Poland Springs
Who kept in his pocket some things.
They'd destroy what they made
Except for a shade,
If that's what the man's will would bring.

There once was another from Duff.
Who had with him similar stuff.
"Uses juices," he said,
"And much neater instead."
But the first man had heard quite enough.

So they took a trip out beyond Mars.
With their fancy and space-worthy cars.
And the man from the Springs
Said, "You'll notice your things
Are as useful as unlit cigars."
*What objects does each man possess?*

### Riddle Teaser 26

 Difficulty: easy

If we stick together we can never be converted.
Unlike those others, when they join, they're sure to
be perverted.
But we can never join with them, for we are sure
to lose.
(It's not because of prejudice, 'tis merely truthful
news.)

There just can be no negative when we show our
power.
And one member of our tribe, he owns the noontide
hour.
We rule almost everywhere, though one more spot
we seek:
If only those dumb humans would add one more day
a week.
*What are we?*

## *Essential*

See if you can make up your own riddle. Think of a
simple object, like a chair, and then write a little rhyme
or limerick about it. If you make it vague and abstract,
but include a few good clues, you've got yourself
a riddle!

## Riddle Teaser 27

 Difficulty: medium

Most machines are bad when hot
Except for the stoves and heaters.
Me, I'm of a different lot
Joined with some other feeders.

For while my job is not to heat,
Heat is what I produce.
But heat production's not my beat
My job is to reduce it.
*What am I?*

## Riddle Teaser 28

 Difficulty: easy

Seven is my lucky number.
So is 21.
Six, it makes me happy, too.
Oh, aren't numbers fun?

Use me for frivolity
Or make a fortune grand.
But I am of no use at all
Unless I leave your hand.
*What am I?*

## Chapter 10
# Science Teasers

These brain-teasers require an understanding of physics, biology, or other sciences. Sometimes specific knowledge is required, but usually intuition is enough.

## Science Teaser 1

 Difficulty: medium

A pirate is floating down a river in a modern sail-boat after having just pillaged a small upstream village. The current is three knots with respect to the land. The wind is zero knots with respect to the land. The pirate wants to proceed downstream as quickly as possible to avoid capture.

Should he raise the sails, or not?

## Science Teaser 2

 Difficulty: medium

NASA has chosen Bobby Braingle to be the first person to visit the planet Venus. On his mission, he will remain in orbit around the planet conducting scientific observations before returning home. During training one day, the mission supervisor approaches Bobby and asks him a simple question. "Bobby, since you are taking great risk in travelling all the way to Venus, I will let you choose the length of your mission. You can stay at Venus for either one day or one year. You decide. Either way, your spacecraft will have enough food and water to sustain you."

Which length of time should Bobby choose if he wants to get back home as soon as possible?

## Science Teaser 3

 Difficulty: medium

You are at a restaurant with your friend when the bill arrives at the table. Your friend, being the clever sort, issues you a challenge. "If you can remove that ice cube from that glass of water without touching the ice, the water, the glass, or the table with your hands, I'll buy you lunch. And to show you that I'm a nice guy, I'll let you use anything on the table." Unfortunately the waiter has already cleared the table and the only things left are the salt and pepper shakers, a little piece of string, and a penny.

How do you remove the ice cube?

## *Essential*

With science teasers, sometimes it helps to think of the extreme cases for a problem. Try to think of the most exaggerated arrangement of the facts that still fits the situation, then see if the problem is easier.

## Science Teaser 4

 Difficulty: easy

What can climb a rope faster than it can go down a rope?

### Science Teaser 5

 Difficulty: easy

You are going on an expedition to the North Pole, and you need to bring along some blankets to keep you warm. You have a choice between a single thick blanket, which is three centimetres thick, and three thin blankets that are each 1 centimetre thick. Which should you choose?

### Science Teaser 6

 Difficulty: medium

Tensile strength is a measure of how well a material resists being pulled apart. In a tug-of-war, for example, you are testing the tensile strength of the rope. Which of the following has a higher tensile strength and why?

- A 6-foot steel rod 1 inch in diameter
- A 6-foot steel cable 1 inch in diameter

### Science Teaser 7

 Difficulty: easy

What is one law of nature that is violated in almost every space battle shown in the movies?

## Science Teaser 8

 Difficulty: medium

In a high school science class, Jimmy is given 50 millilitres of water and 50 millilitres of ethanol. His task is to mix them together and then run a certain experiment on the mixture. When the teacher comes to check on him, however, Jimmy's mixture only measures 94 millilitres. The teacher accuses him of drinking some of the mixture and immediately sends him to the principal. Jimmy swears that he did not drink the mixture and that he didn't lose any of the liquids by any means. What happened to the other six millilitres, and how can Jimmy prove his innocence?

## Science Teaser 9

 Difficulty: medium

You have a rubber balloon with a string attached to it. A weight is attached to the other end of the string. You fill the balloon with enough air so that if you submerge it and the weight in water to a depth of 30 feet, the balloon will neither rise nor sink – with its buoyancy exactly balanced by gravity. You then pull the balloon and weight down another 30 feet. If you let the balloon go at this depth, will it rise or sink? (Assume that the water temperature is the same at both depths.)

### Science Teaser 10

 Difficulty: easy

Steven Wright, an American comedian, has a famous one-liner: "I just bought some powdered water, but I didn't know what to add." While this is a funny line, it should be obvious to Mr. Wright what he needs to add. What is it?

### Science Teaser 11

 Difficulty: easy

NASA is on a mission to collect dust from the moon's surface. A team is put together to design an apparatus that an astronaut can use to accomplish this task. One member of the team designs a type of vacuum cleaner to suck up and collect the dust. He is immediately fired for his incompetence. What is wrong with his plan?

### Science Teaser 12

 Difficulty: hard

A scientist in his lab brings pure water to a boil. Then, without cooling the water or donning any kind of protective clothing, he immediately pours the water onto his head without scalding himself. How does he do it?

## Science Teaser 13

 Difficulty: easy

Professor Lipshultz is showing off his new inventions to a prospective investor. He tells the investor that he had developed four machines that will allow scientists to study the motion of gas molecules. His explanation of how the machines work together goes as follows:

"The first unit will take in any gas and completely dry it, removing all traces of water. Right now it is removing water vapor from air . . . and now you can see the 'DRY' light has come on.

The second unit removes all but one molecule from the chamber. There you see the 'READY' light, indicating that only a single molecule remains.

The third unit analyzes the contents of the chamber, determining exactly what chemicals are in the chamber, and in what quantity. And as you can see on the screen, the unit indicates 'Air: 1 molecule.'

The final machine will trace the path that the molecule takes as it bounces around the chamber. The path is represented by the lines on this computer screen."

"I'm sorry," said the investor, "but you're obviously lying to me. I can accept the fact that three of the four machines *could* work as you say, but one of them is obviously a fake."

Which machine was the fake?

### Science Teaser 14

 Difficulty: easy

Many years ago, a scientist decided to try an experiment to determine the speed of light. He had his assistant stand at one end of a beach with a powerful torch, and the scientist stood at the other end, 500 yards away, with a stopwatch. The assistant would raise his hand and turn on the torch at the same time. The scientist would time the difference between when he saw the assistant's hand and when he saw the light, and would calculate the speed of light knowing the distance between them. Now we all know that light travels too quickly for the scientist to measure a difference with a stopwatch. However, even if light travelled very slowly the experiment would still have failed. Why?

### Science Teaser 15

 Difficulty: medium

Normally, when you put an ice-cube into a glass of water it clings to the edge of the glass. How can you make the ice-cube float near the centre of the glass?

### Science Teaser 16

 Difficulty: medium

Tight-rope walkers frequently carry a long pole to help them balance. Why does this help?

## Science Teaser 17

 Difficulty: hard

Bobby Braingle is having a birthday party in the back of a limousine. He has a helium balloon that he holds by its string. Suddenly, the driver swerves to the right to avoid hitting a dog. As a result of the sharp turn, Bobby is flung to the left. Which way does his balloon go?

## Science Teaser 18

 Difficulty: hard

Dimwit Dan is hiking in the woods when he comes across a giant hive of bees that start chasing him. Dan quickly turns around and runs toward the lake that he has just passed. He remembers from old cartoons that you can hide under the water and breathe through a reed or hollow tube. He happens to be carrying a hollow walking stick, so he jumps into the lake and swims to the bottom. He pokes his walking stick up to the surface and starts breathing. Unfortunately for Dan, he dies after a few minutes. Why?

## Science Teaser 19

 Difficulty: easy

If you wanted to wrap a rope around the entire earth and tie it very tight so that nothing could squeeze between the rope and the ground, you would need a very long rope. Now, suppose you added 3 feet to the length of the rope. How much of a gap would you have between the earth and the rope?

## Science Teaser 20

 Difficulty: medium

You have applied to become a member of the Elite Chemists Society. After many gruelling interviews and tests, your membership approval comes down to the final challenge. You are put in a room whose walls are lined with containers. Each container is filled with a specific element from the periodic table of elements. One container has iron, another has argon gas, and so on, with all of the elements represented. In the middle of the room is a clear tube 4 feet high and 1 inch in diameter. At the bottom of the tube is a steel ball 0.9 inches in diameter. You must get the ball out of the tube without breaking or picking up the tube, and you may only use the raw elements contained in the room. How do you do it?

## Science Teaser 21

 Difficulty: medium

Which of these glass containers is more likely to crack when you pour hot boiling water into it: a thin wineglass or a thick beer mug?

## Science Teaser 22

 Difficulty: easy

Hydrogen is very flammable, as you may know from hearing about the *Hindenburg* disaster. Suppose you held your breath and went into a room filled with 100 percent hydrogen gas and then struck a match. What would happen?

## Science Teaser 23

 Difficulty: easy

Airplanes can travel at 400 miles per hour. Bobby Braingle owns a bird that has flown at 410 miles per hour. How is this possible?

## *Fact*

Here are two simple equations that might be useful for solving some science brain-teasers:

Distance = Velocity ÷ Time (where rate is constant)

Velocity = Acceleration ÷ Time (where velocity is constant and object starts at rest)

### Science Teaser 24

 Difficulty: hard

If you have a container of air and you double the amount of air in the container, the new pressure will be double the old pressure. Let's say you measure the air pressure in your tyres. The gauge reads with the standard pressure, 32 pounds per square inch (psi). If you were to double the amount of air in the tyre without causing the tyre to expand in any way, what pressure would your tyre gauge read then? The answer is NOT 64 psi.

### Science Teaser 25

 Difficulty: hard

You are in a sweet shop, and you want to buy a Jumbo Jawbreaker. You notice that there is a contest currently being run on Jawbreakers. One in every five Jawbreakers has a hollow centre. If you get a hollow Jawbreaker, you will win $10. Without breaking open any of the Jawbreakers, how can you cheat and make sure you only purchase a hollow one?

### Science Teaser 26

 Difficulty: easy

If you have no air-conditioning, would leaving your refrigerator door open cool off your kitchen?

## Science Teaser 27

 Difficulty: medium

You have two identical party balloons. You blow one up 80 percent full and another you blow up 40 percent full. Now you attach the two balloons together at the mouth so that the air can flow between the two balloons. What will happen?

a. Nothing will happen.
b. The balloons will equalise so they are the same size.
c. The small balloon will give all its air to the large balloon.
d. The large balloon will give all its air to the small balloon.

## *Essential*

Don't worry if you didn't take a lot of science classes in school – these teasers aren't nearly as difficult as your end of term exams. Many of these teasers are based on a single principle or fact that you probably remember from physics or chemistry lessons.

## Science Teaser 28

 Difficulty: medium

What will happen to a raisin if you put it into a glass of soda?

## Chapter 11
# Series Teasers

The following teasers give you a list of numbers, letters, or words. It's up to you to work out the rules that determine the sequence and what the next number, letter, or word would be.

### Series Teaser 1

⚠ Difficulty: easy

Bobby recently bought a 10-volume set of encyclopedias. At present, he has only arranged the first eight volumes on his shelf, in the order shown below:

8, 5, 4, 1, 7, 6, 3, 2

Using Bobby's system, where should volumes 9 and 10 go?

### Series Teaser 2

⚠ Difficulty: medium

What is the last letter of this series?

EPAYNNVASIDEPASNNEAEYENR?

### Series Teaser 3

⚠ Difficulty: hard

Why are these words in this order?

BASH, ALE, ABLE, EAR, BONY

## Series Teaser 4

 Difficulty: hard

What is the next letter in this series?

H, B, C, N, O, F, P, S, ?

## Series Teaser 5

 Difficulty: medium

What is the next letter in this series?

A, B, G, D, E, Z, E, T, ?

## Series Teaser 6

 Difficulty: easy

What is the next number?

123,456,789; 45; 9; 9; 9; ?

## Series Teaser 7

 Difficulty: medium

What is the next name?

John, John, Chester, James, George, George, Jimmy, ?

### Series Teaser 8

 Difficulty: easy

Why are these countries listed in this order?

> Russia, Canada, United States, China, Brazil,
> Australia, India, Argentina

### Series Teaser 9

 Difficulty: easy

What is the next time in this sequence?

> 1:06, 2:11, 3:17, 4:22, 5:28, 6:33, 7:38, 8:44, ?

### Series Teaser 10

 Difficulty: easy

What is the next number in this series?

> 2, 3, 10, 12, 13, 20, 21, ?

### Series Teaser 11

 Difficulty: medium

Which letters go in the missing spot?

> Me, Ve, ??, Ju, Sa, Ur, Ne, Pl

## Series Teaser 12

 Difficulty: easy

The first animal in this series is missing. Can you work out which one it is?

   ?, BAT, CHEETAH, DONKEY, ELEPHANT, FISH, GOAT

   Your choices are:

a. Zebra
b. Shark
c. Horse
d. Ant-eater

## Series Teaser 13

 Difficulty: medium

What is significant about the order of these letters?

   RKBQKBKR

## Series Teaser 14

 Difficulty: easy

What is the missing symbol, and where in this series does it go?

   !@#$^&*

## *Essential*

When trying to solve a series problem, it helps to remember the frequently used methods of ordering things. Are the items in alphabetical or numerical order? Are they grouped by size, length, height, or age?

## Series Teaser 15

⚠ Difficulty: medium

What is the last letter in this sequence?

T, H, E, R, A, T, E, N, ?

## Series Teaser 16

⚠ Difficulty: medium

Which word could go into the missing spot?
DOLLAR, REMIX, MISSING, FATHER, ? ,
LATER, TIRED, DO

Here are your options:

a. North
b. South
c. East
d. West

## Series Teaser 17

 Difficulty: hard

What is the next number?

2, 7, 17, 37, 77, 157, ?

## Series Teaser 18

 Difficulty: easy

What is the next word in this list?

RUN, GLUE, FREE, CORE, DIVE, PICKS, ?

## Series Teaser 19

 Difficulty: hard

What are the missing items in this series?

?, 15, 30, 40, ?

## Series Teaser 20

 Difficulty: medium

Bobby Braingle ran several errands. First, he went to the police station to retrieve something from Lost Property. Then he went to the market to buy some apples before dropping his car off with the mechanic. He then stopped at the DIY shop for some paint for his kitchen. Of the following choices, what was his next and final stop before reaching home?

a. Pet shop
b. Sweet factory
c. Pizza place
d. First International Bank of Puzzleonia

## Series Teaser 21

 Difficulty: easy

What is the last word in this sentence?

The five boxing wizards jump _____.

## Series Teaser 22

 Difficulty: easy

What are the next two numbers in this series?

2, 3, 5, 7, 11, 13, 17, 19, 23, 29, ?, ?

## Series Teaser 23

 Difficulty: medium

Why are these cities ordered in this way?

KABUL, BUENOS AIRES, CANBERRA,
VIENNA, BRUSSELS, ROME, MOSCOW

## *Fact*

If you suspect that a series is mathematical in nature,
start by calculating the difference between each number.
Sometimes you will see a pattern within the differences.

## Series Teaser 24

 Difficulty: hard

One letter is missing from the end of this series. What is it
and why?

A, E, H, I, K, L, M, N, O, P, U, ?

## Series Teaser 25

 Difficulty: medium

The numbers below form the beginning of an infinite
series. Can you list the next few numbers?

1, 4, 1, 5, 9, 2, 6, 5, 3, 5

## Series Teaser 26

⚠ Difficulty: medium

Which letter is last in this tricky sequence?

W, L, I, L, I, T, T, ?

## Chapter 12
# Situational Teasers

In a situational puzzle, you or someone else is put in an imaginary situation, and you must work out what to do. You will need to use various techniques, including common sense and logic, to arrive at the answer. Some situational puzzles are not designed to be solved by a single person. These puzzles are called lateral-thinking puzzles and will be described later in this chapter.

## Situational Teaser 1

 Difficulty: easy

One night while working at the recycling plant, Bobby receives an unexpected and frantic telephone call from a neighbour. After listening to the neighbour's rant, Bobby slams down the phone, leaves work, and drives straight home as fast as he can. When he arrives, Bobby creeps upstairs. Upon entering the bedroom, he finds his wife in bed with a stranger.

Surprisingly, he isn't angry. In fact Bobby, actually tiptoes downstairs and makes his wife some breakfast. He then takes it up for her so she can eat it in bed.

Why is Bobby so calm about finding his wife in bed with someone he has never met?

## Situational Teaser 2

 Difficulty: medium

You have a correctly set analogue wall clock with marks to indicate the hours but no numbers. You can only see the clock through a mirror. To complicate things, it is installed upside down.

When you look in the mirror, you see that the time appears to be 7:55 (although the hour hand is just a little bit away from where it's supposed to be). What is the real time?

## Situational Teaser 3

 Difficulty: hard

You are working in a lab. For the experiment you want to complete, you need to set a beaker of water on a surface exactly 17 inches above the table. Besides the beaker, the only objects in the lab are a yardstick and five phone books, which are 1 inch, 3 inches, 4 inches, 5 inches, and 6 inches thick respectively.

How do you arrange the books so that you can set the beaker at the correct height?

## Situational Teaser 4

 Difficulty: easy

A small boy throws a tennis ball 50 feet. It turns around in mid-flight and returns to the boy. How does this happen?

## Situational Teaser 5

 Difficulty: medium

A scuba diver is 200 feet under water. He swims around a corner and sees a full-grown, although dead, pine tree rooted to the ground. How did the tree grow here, 200 feet under water?

## Situational Teaser 6

 Difficulty: easy

Bobby Braingle's brother Robby, who doesn't like what passes for art these days, runs into the National Gallery and causes millions of dollars' worth of damage to several masterpieces. Later that day, Robby is invited to meet the manager and is warmly thanked for his actions. Why is the manager so happy with him?

## Situational Teaser 7

 Difficulty: medium

An 18-wheeler is wedged between the ground and a low bridge. The driver failed to realized that his lorry is 1 inch too high to pass under the bridge. How can the driver get the lorry out?

## Situational Teaser 8

 Difficulty: medium

Bobby Braingle returns to his car after a good film and notices that one of his tyres has been stolen. The crooks jacked up his car and stole the entire tyre, including the hubcap and all four lug nuts. Luckily Bobby has a spare in the trunk, but he doesn't have any spare nuts. How does he attach the spare?

## Situational Teaser 9

 Difficulty: medium

Bobby is at the races. Ten horses are running in the current race. Bobby has a piece of paper with the name of the winning horse printed on it, yet when the race is over he finds he bet on a losing horse. What happened?

## Situational Teaser 10

 Difficulty: medium

A bank robber runs into a bank. A few minutes later he runs out with £10,000 stashed in a bag. A police officer who saw the whole thing doesn't raise a finger. Why not?

## Situational Teaser 11

 Difficulty: medium

How would you pick up exactly one teaspoon of sugar using only your fingers and no measuring instruments?

## Situational Teaser 12

 Difficulty: easy

You have just discovered that there is a fly in your coffee. You want to send it back, but you know that the waiters at this restaurant have a reputation for being surly. You worry that your waiter will simply remove the fly and give you the same coffee. What can you do so that you will know if you have a fresh cup of coffee?

### Situational Teaser 13

 Difficulty: medium

Professor Braingle gives his class a test. Half of the students in the class turn their tests over and don't answer any questions. The other half of the students answer all the questions. When the results are passed back, all the students who wrote nothing passed while the students who wrote answers failed. Why?

## *Essential*

Lateral-thinking situational teasers cannot be solved by one person. They are designed to be a group activity. One person should read the teaser out loud to the group and then read the answer silently. The rest of the group must guess the answer by asking the leader yes-or-no questions.

### Situational Teaser 14

 Difficulty: medium

A man hears a familiar noise. He calls the police, and a man is arrested. Why?

### Situational Teaser 15

 Difficulty: medium

A man drops more than 1,000 feet to the ground without a parachute, but he walks away unharmed. How?

## Situational Teaser 16

 Difficulty: easy

A man walks outside to pick up the morning paper. When he comes back inside he is sunburned. He was only outside for a few minutes, so how did he get sunburned?

## Situational Teaser 17

 Difficulty: easy

There is a very prestigious race with a prize of £100,000 for the winner. A runner won the race but didn't get a penny of the prize money. Why?

## Situational Teaser 18

 Difficulty: medium

A woman hears a gunshot in the next room, yet she doesn't do anything. She just keeps reading her book. Why?

## Situational Teaser 19

 Difficulty: medium

Two cars are in a minor traffic accident, and nobody is hurt. When the police arrive, the man in the back of one of the cars is dead. How?

### Situational Teaser 20

 Difficulty: medium

Inspector Bobby Braingle arrives at a crime scene and sees the body of a woman hanging from the ceiling. Below her body is an upturned chair.

"It's a suicide," a constable informs Inspector Bobby. "She stood on this chair here and then kicked it away."

"I think," replied Inspector Bobby, "that you are incorrect. This is a murder."

How did he know it wasn't a suicide?

### Situational Teaser 21

 Difficulty: medium

A man is lying on the beach. The tide comes in, and he drowns. Why didn't he get up before the water got too high?

### Situational Teaser 22

 Difficulty: hard

A man drops a brick. He doesn't intend to hurt himself, but within a minute his nose is broken. How?

### Situational Teaser 23

 Difficulty: medium

Hank and Wanda are lying dead in the middle of the floor. Broken glass and little rocks are strewn around the room. How did they die?

### Situational Teaser 24

 Difficulty: easy

A carrot, a few stones, and some sticks are lying on the ground. Why?

### Situational Teaser 25

 Difficulty: easy

An unhappy couple hires a man to shoot them. The man takes their money and shoots them several times. Later, the couple goes home happy. How did they survive?

### Situational Teaser 26

 Difficulty: hard

A man takes off his hat. A few minutes later he is dead. Why?

### Situational Teaser 27

Difficulty: easy

On most days, Bobby drives home from work and parks right in front of his house. However, on Thursdays, Bobby parks two streets away and walks home. Why?

## *Essential*

> Try to resist the urge to give hints if you are the clue giver. It's much more fun if the question-askers get to work out the solution on their own.

### Situational Teaser 28

 Difficulty: medium

A man has just purchased a piano for his flat. The only way to get it up the five flights of stairs is to rent a crane to lift it through the window. Unluckily, as he is lifting the piano off the ground, a cable snaps. The piano falls and lands on top of the man. A few moments later, the man is unharmed and looking disappointedly at his broken piano. How did he not get harmed?

## Chapter 13
# Trick Teasers

Trick teasers appear difficult at first, but once you work out the trick they become easy. Be creative, and don't give up too quickly. Sometimes the answer requires a different interpretation of the teaser.

### Trick Teaser 1

 Difficulty: medium

A Puzzleonia train leaves the city of Slowville and heads for Quicksville, some 400 miles away. At the same time, Bobby Braingle sets off for Quicksville in his vintage motorcar, travelling at the same speed as the train. Unbeknownst to Bobby, his motorcar had developed four slow punctures – one in each tyre. By the time he has completed three-quarters of the journey, Bobby's car tyres are completely flat. Bobby does not change his tyres anywhere along the way, but he still arrives in Quicksville at the same moment as the train. How can this be possible?

### Trick Teaser 2

 Difficulty: easy

Which weighs more, a ton of 2-ounce cotton balls or a ton of 10-pound gold bricks?

### Trick Teaser 3

 Difficulty: medium

You have a glass of water with seven ice-cubes floating in it. Each ice-cube is 1 inch square. When the ice melts, will you have more or less water in the glass, assuming you don't drink any?

### Trick Teaser 4

 Difficulty: easy

Imagine you are in a cage whose bars are 2 inches apart. There is only one door but it is locked. On the floor are a saucer of water and a bale of straw. There is a very hungry lion in the cage with you. How will you survive?

### Trick Teaser 5

 Difficulty: hard

What is half of 8 but not twice 2?

### Trick Teaser 6

 Difficulty: medium

Captain Kirk has been captured by the evil Braingaloids. They bring him before the Big Braingaloid, who says to him:

"Captain Kirk, you are accused of meddling in our affairs. You may make one statement, but beware. If your statement is false, you will be fed to the lions. If your statement is true, you will be buried alive. If you don't say anything or if we can't verify your statement, you will be forced to drink poison. If your statement is not a statement or is a paradox, we will toss you into a pool of acid."

What should Captain Kirk say to get out of this mess?

### Trick Teaser 7

 Difficulty: easy

Mandy can spell her name with only two letters. How?

### Trick Teaser 8

 Difficulty: hard

Working with only four toothpicks, can you arrange them so that they form a shape that contains a triangle and a square? You cannot break any of the toothpicks.

### Trick Teaser 9

 Difficulty: medium

How can 6 be half of 11?

### Trick Teaser 10

Difficulty: easy

The President of the United States, the Pope, and a big movie star are in an airplane. There is only one parachute. The President says, "I run the strongest country in the world and my death would be mourned by millions. I should get the parachute." The Pope says, "I have helped millions of people, but I am old and I have lived life well." The movie star says, "I entertain millions of people and I have two young children to look after. I need the parachute." Who will survive?

### Trick Teaser 11

 Difficulty: easy

What can you subtract from 7 so that the answer is even? The number you subtract cannot be odd.

### Trick Teaser 12

 Difficulty: medium

Three monkeys are sitting in a tree. Two decides to climb down. How many are left in the tree?

### Trick Teaser 13

 Difficulty: easy

Bobby is in jail, talking with his lawyer. He has been arrested for tax fraud and it doesn't look good. Fortunately, this jail has good food and they treat the prisoners nicely. After Bobby and his lawyer finish talking, Bobby says something to the guard and is allowed to leave. What does he say?

### Trick Teaser 14

 Difficulty: medium

When do you have the best odds at winning a game of bingo, 12:50 P.M. or 12:55 P.M.?

### Trick Teaser 15

 Difficulty: medium

Robin, Hilary, Amber, and Kim are all friends on the same volleyball team. After a game, they all decide to change clothes and go get some ice-cream. Amber goes off and changes by herself before meeting her friends outside the gym. Why?

### Trick Teaser 16

 Difficulty: medium

Keiko was born and raised in Japan. As everyone knows, only the United States celebrates Independence Day; however, Keiko always has a party to celebrate the Fourth of July. Why?

### Trick Teaser 17

 Difficulty: easy

Let's say you have $300. You go to the grocery store and take 15 pounds of apples that cost $2.23 per pound. How much money do you have left?

### Trick Teaser 18

 Difficulty: hard

If you multiply the number of toes on each foot of each person in Australia, what number do you get?

## Trick Teaser 19

 Difficulty: hard

Bobby and Phyllis are avid poker players. They are playing a game, when all of a sudden Phyllis gets an ace and wins. Bobby never looks at any cards. How does Phyllis know that she has won?

## Trick Teaser 20

 Difficulty: easy

What has 18 feet and can play baseball?

## Trick Teaser 21

 Difficulty: medium

A shepherd has three sheep on one acre of grassy land. Each sheep can eat 2 square feet of grass a day. How long will it take the sheep to eat all of the grass?

## Trick Teaser 22

 Difficulty: medium

Bobby Braingle is starving, but he can't leave for lunch until he finishes the budget report for tomorrow's meeting. Bobby notices that he has an apple on his desk, yet he doesn't eat it. Why not?

### Trick Teaser 23

 Difficulty: easy

Certain coins become very valuable, while other coins remain at face value. Why are 1976 quarters minted in Philadelphia worth almost £500?

### Trick Teaser 24

Difficulty: hard

Bobby is a newspaper columnist. Unfortunately, his alarm clock failed to go off and he overslept. As a chronic procrastinator, Bobby now has 10 minutes to write a 1,000-word column. How will he ever finish?

### Trick Teaser 25

 Difficulty: hard

Bobby looks out his kitchen window and witnesses a murder, yet nobody has died. How is this possible?

### Trick Teaser 26

 Difficulty: easy

You are locked in the back of a car. The only thing you have is a pocketknife, a shoelace, and a half-eaten chocolate bar. How do you get out?

### Trick Teaser 27

 Difficulty: easy

What doesn't belong?

WHICH, WHAT, WHEN, WHERE, WHY, BANANA

### Trick Teaser 28

 Difficulty: medium

Bobby goes to the zoo and sees lots of animals. He notices that at least one animal drinks with its eyes. Which animal was this?

## Alert!

The title of this chapter is a pretty big hint that normal reasoning is not the way to solve these puzzles. After you've solved them, try these out on a friend, and don't tell them it's a trick. It's always fun to see your friends squirm.

## *Chapter 14*
# **Trivia Teasers**

This final group of brain-teasers all require some specific knowledge in order to find the solution. To solve them, get ready to pull out those trivia facts you've got stored in your brain. You're also likely to need to use maths, logic, or some other technique from a previous chapter.

## Trivia Teaser 1

 Difficulty: hard

Inspector Bobby Braingle is a collector of rare and unusual coins. On a visit to a nearby market, he comes upon a stall selling collectible coins. The stall is run by the well-known female villain Maude Upname. Inspector Bobby browses the contents of her stall, looking at several interesting commemorative coins celebrating 100 Years of Puzzles. Maude Upname sees Inspector Bobby's interest and decides to offer him a special coin she has been saving.

"It's a special one-of-a-kind coin," she tells Bobby. "It was minted to celebrate the birth of Queen Elizabeth the Second." Inspector Bobby views the coin and reads the inscription on its reverse side. It says, "In celebration of the birth of Princess Elizabeth, daughter to the Duke and Duchess of York, heir to the throne of the United Kingdom and the colonies of the Empire."

"Where did you get this?" asks Inspector Bobby.

"It was given to my grandmother in 1926, the year of the Queen's birth. It's 100 percent genuine, honest, I swear on it."

"Well, in that case, you are under arrest for forgery!" the inspector cries.

How did Bobby know the coin was a fake?

## Trivia Teaser 2

 Difficulty: medium

Below are four verses that sound like they could come from a famous Beatles song, if the title were taken literally. For example, a song about a calendar that's all messed up would fit nicely with the title "*Eight Days a Week.*" Can you determine which titles these verses are referring to?

1. Yup, there she was
   Not doing very much.
   Not sitting or lying
   Or anything of the such.

2. You pulled the ball from Charlie's kick.
   You flew up in the air.
   You hoarded all my jewellery, girl
   And that just isn't fair.

3. I walk just fine, just fine I do,
   When underneath the moon.
   But when the sun comes out, my friend,
   I stumble like a goon.

### Trivia Teaser 3

⚠ Difficulty: hard

What is the missing word in this group? (The following words are in no particular order.)

> SCAPHOID, LUNATE, TRIQUETRUM, PISIFORM, TRAPEZIUM, TRAPEZOID, CAPITATE

### Trivia Teaser 4

⚠ Difficulty: medium

Bobby Braingle recounts the details of a hunting trip to entertain a bunch of his buddies. "We were deep in the Amazon, when all of a sudden a 10-foot alligator jumped into our boat. After about 15 minutes of wrestling, I strangled the gator, and now I have this trophy on my wall."

After hearing this, an acquaintance spoke up, "That story is completely made up, you liar!"

How did the acquaintance know?

### Trivia Teaser 5

⚠ Difficulty: hard

The following maths equation is true under a very special circumstance. What is it?

11 + 8 + 8 = 17

### Trivia Teaser 6

 Difficulty: hard

A group of dogs is called a pack, and a group of cows is called a herd. Do you know what a group of the following animals are called?

1. Buzzards
2. Cobras
3. Turtles
4. Sharks

### Trivia Teaser 7

 Difficulty: medium

Many books tell the story of someone who single-handedly murdered one quarter of the earth's population. What was this person's name?

### Trivia Teaser 8

 Difficulty: hard

If you wrote down the first letter of every country in the world, you will have written every letter at least once except for the letter X. Most of the letters will be on your list multiple times. Which letters are only written once, and which countries do they represent?

### Trivia Teaser 9

 Difficulty: hard

What comes next in this series?

88, 225, 365, 687, ?

### Trivia Teaser 10

 Difficulty: medium

Bobby Braingle is playing a game of golf with his boss. Bobby is not a very good golfer, and on the second hole, he hits his ball into a bunker. His boss, who is very skilled, hits his ball onto the green. When Bobby arrives at the bunker, he notices that there are two golf balls in the bunker. Both are face down so he cannot identify which one is his. What should he do so as not to incur a penalty?

### Trivia Teaser 11

 Difficulty: easy

A professor is giving a lecture to his students. He says, "Albert Einstein and Stephen Hawking are two of the smartest physicists of our time. In a historic meeting, they argued about Einstein's theory of relativity. Hawking said that it was too complicated and that it could be simplified. In spite of this, they remained friends." A student raised his hand, "Professor, I'm sorry, but you are clearly making this up." How did the student know?

## *Essential*

If you can't get enough trivia, check out the Web site *www.funtrivia.com*. It contains thousands of quizzes on many different topics. It even features a trivia tournament, where you can win prizes.

### Trivia Teaser 12

 Difficulty: medium

Vera Dangerous was one of the worst female criminals of all time. When she was arrested in California in 1954, she was accused and convicted of 17 murders. For the last 30 years, incorrigible murderers had been sent to Alcatraz Island, but Vera was not sent there. Why not? (Alcatraz didn't close until 1963.)

### Trivia Teaser 13

 Difficulty: easy

Crocodile Pete is famous for his tall tales of hunting expeditions. One day in a local Sydney bar, he is recalling his last adventure during his Christmas trip to Argentina. He had been building a snowman, when all of a sudden a wild dog jumped out and attacked him. After wrestling for 15 minutes, he was able to subdue the dog. Everyone in the bar instantly knew that he was lying. How did they know?

### Trivia Teaser 14

 Difficulty: hard

Who is missing from this group?

KLEIO, EUTERPE, THALEIA, MELPOMENE,
TERPSICHORE, ERATO, POLYMNIA, OURANIA

### Trivia Teaser 15

 Difficulty: easy

Which are the only two countries whose names start with
A that don't also end with A?

### Trivia Teaser 16

 Difficulty: medium

Bobby Braingle has come up with a great idea for getting
the ice off of his windscreen. He wants to boil a bucket
of washer fluid and dump it on the windscreen. This, he
reckons, will quickly melt the ice and clean his windows
at the same time. Why is this a bad idea?

### Trivia Teaser 17

 Difficulty: hard

Most people have heard about plants like the Venus fly-
trap or pitcher plant that eat flies for nutrients instead of
getting their food from the ground. Are there any plants
that can move around, instead of being stuck in place?

## Trivia Teaser 18

 Difficulty: hard

Finishing this series of percentages is relatively easy, but what do these values represent?

30%, 20.3%, 16.3%, 8.9%, 8.9%, 6.7%, 5.2%, ?

## Trivia Teaser 19

 Difficulty: hard

Bobby Braingle comes into the doctor's office complaining of being sleep-deprived. "I don't know what it is, doctor. I always fall asleep shortly after sundown, and I awake with the sunrise, but over the last few weeks I have been getting more and more tired. Can you prescribe me something?" What does the doctor do?

## Trivia Teaser 20

 Difficulty: easy

Bobby is scuba-diving with his buddy, Nobby. They are exploring the Great Barrier Reef off the coast of Australia. All of a sudden, a big eel jumps out from behind a rock and swims right between Bobby and Nobby. Both of them are a little startled, but the eel swims away and they are both left unharmed. Bobby turns to his friend and gives him the "ok" signal with his fingers. His buddy then gives Bobby the "thumbs up" signal. What do they do next?

### Trivia Teaser 21

⚠ Difficulty: medium

Which animal from Group A belongs in Group B?

A. Ape, peacock, crocodile, rabbit, salmon
B. Giraffe, elephant, lion, poodle, mouse

## *Essential*

Don't be afraid to use reference materials to solve trivia teasers. Each of these puzzles requires knowledge of certain facts that aren't necessarily common sense. If you know what the puzzle is getting at, but you don't know the necessary facts by heart, go ahead and look them up!

# Answers

## Answers to Quickie Teasers

**Answer to Quickie Teaser 1**
Peace on Earth

**Answer to Quickie Teaser 2**
Jumping for joy

**Answer to Quickie Teaser 3**
All the words are palindromes (spelled the same forward and backward). Any other palindrome will work, such as "noon" or "racecar."

**Answer to Quickie Teaser 4**
CHEESE does not belong because it does not come from a plant.

**Answer to Quickie Teaser 5**
24 hours = 1 day

**Answer to Quickie Teaser 6**
Snow White and the 7 Dwarves

**Answer to Quickie Teaser 7**
The pool doesn't have any water in it.

**Answer to Quickie Teaser 8**
Light the fuse at both ends or in the middle, and it will burn in both directions at once (and in half the time).

**Answer to Quickie Teaser 9**
The son has a 6-foot shadow.

**Answer to Quickie Teaser 10**
Thirteen apples are in the basket.

**Answer to Quickie Teaser 11**
The answer is 1.

**Answer to Quickie Teaser 12**
Two years ago, when Sparky was ten and Snowball was five.

**Answer to Quickie Teaser 13**
9,841

**Answer to Quickie Teaser 14**
The probability is 50/50. Each coin toss is an independent event and has the same odds as the others. That is, past tosses have no effect on the probability of future flips. It is just a coincidence that it came up heads 10 times in a row.

**Answer to Quickie Teaser 15**
Zero. It's impossible to correctly label only three cans, because if three are correct, the fourth label must also be on the correct can.

**Answer to Quickie Teaser 16**
First, cook it. Then bend it. Then let it dry.

**Answer to Quickie Teaser 17**
1,024. Each number in the series is the previous number multiplied by four.

**Answer to Quickie Teaser 18**
SN. All the other items are directions on a compass.

**Answer to Quickie Teaser 19**
You see nothing because you are blindfolded.

**Answer to Quickie Teaser 20**
The next item would be F (the symbol for the element fluorine).

These are the elements of the periodic table in order.

## Answer to Quickie Teaser 21
Dihydrogen monoxide is another word for water ($H_2O$).

## Answer to Quickie Teaser 22
You should take the penny. Work out how much all those doublings would total with the simple formula $xy^z$. Here, $x$ = the original amount (1 penny), $y$ = the rate by which your money will increase (double, or 2), and $z$ = the number of days it is doubled (let's say 30). That gives us $1 \times 2^{30}$, or $10,737,418.24.

## Answer to Quickie Teaser 23
The cheap doll is 50 pence, and the expensive doll is £100.50. Together they cost £101.

## Answer to Quickie Teaser 24
Because you have no aunts, your uncle's brother-in-law must be your father.

## Answer to Quickie Teaser 25
There are six possible outcomes for each roll. In three of them you win, and in three of them you lose, so it's a fair challenge.

## Answer to Quickie Teaser 26
A book.

## Answer to Quickie Teaser 27
The answer is WHEAT. Cheese comes from a cow, while flour comes from wheat.

## Answer to Quickie Teaser 28
E (for "eight"). This series is made up of the first letter of the numbers one, two, three, and so on.

## Answers to Group Teasers

## Answer to Group Teaser 1
GLK does not belong. All the other letter groups are made up of keys that are adjacent on a standard keyboard.

## Answer to Group Teaser 2
TNLKAZY are letters that can be drawn with straight lines. RQOJGDS are letters that can be drawn with curvy lines.

## Answer to Group Teaser 3
Sentence 4 does not belong. In all the other sentences, the first letters of each word spell the name of a fruit: apple, banana, and kiwi.

## Answer to Group Teaser 4
TEE and UNDER must be swapped. The words in Group 1 remain words when you add "th" to the end (hearTH, breadTH, elevenTH, teeTH). The words in Group 2 remain words when you add "th" to the beginning (THinks, THread, THeatre, THunder).

## Answer to Group Teaser 5
All the words can be created from the letters in the word TEASER.

### Answer to Group Teaser 6

The letter J would go in Group 1. The letters in Group 1 go below the line when written in lower case, while the letters in Group 2 don't.

### Answer to Group Teaser 7

ENLIST. All are six-letter words using the letters I, S, T, E, N, and L.

### Answer to Group Teaser 8

The letter Q belongs in Group 2. The letters in Group 1 are open (that is, they include no closed areas). The letters in Group 2 do include closed area(s).

### Answer to Group Teaser 9

If you were to put all 50 states in alphabetical order and number them, you would see that the selected states all correspond to prime numbers.

### Answer to Group Teaser 10

Each word has a number spelled backward inside it: ENOugh, blOWTorch, marXISt, mENINgitis, NETtle.

### Answer to Group Teaser 11

CHEESE does not belong. The others all have homonyms (aunt, week, rowed, paws, bury), but there is no other word that sounds the same as "cheese."

### Answer to Group Teaser 12

BEEF belongs in the group because it too can be spelled

from among the first seven letters of the alphabet.

### Answer to Group Teaser 13

All of the words are synonyms of words that sound like numbers: won (one), too (two), fore (four), ate (eight), sics (six).

### Answer to Group Teaser 14

JURY, TENT, VOICE and TENSE belong in the inbox; with the addition of the prefix "in," each one makes a new word (injury, intent, invoice, intense). LINE, BACK, BURST, and CRY belong in the outbox because they make new words with the addition of the prefix "out" (outline, outback, outburst, outcry).

### Answer to Group Teaser 15

Each item in the list is a movie title with all its vowels removed: *Casablanca, The Godfather, The Wizard of Oz,* and *It's a Wonderful Life.*

### Answer to Group Teaser 16

You can find them all at the zoo. Each word is the scrambled name of an animal: gorilla, giraffe, elephant, cheetah, ostrich.

### Answer to Group Teaser 17

Steve is married to Kathy. The bride's and groom's names have a total of 10 letters combined.

**Answer to Group Teaser 18**
Hg does not belong. On the periodic table, it is the symbol for mercury (element 80), which is a metalloid. All the other symbols are for lanthanoids (elements 57 through 70).

**Answer to Group Teaser 19**
12. It is the only number in the group that isn't a teen.

**Answer to Group Teaser 20**
They are the first letters in the names of Santa's reindeer: Dasher, Dancer, Prancer, Vixen, Comet, Cupid, Donner, and Blitzen.

**Answer to Group Teaser 21**
Dog owners have names that start with a vowel. Cat owners have names that end with a vowel. Emma has a vowel at both the beginning and the end of her name, so she would own both a cat and a dog.

**Answer to Group Teaser 22**
Each word contains one of the numeric prefixes, in numeric order: TRIck, sQUAD, serPENT, catHEXis, antiSEPTic, and OCTopus.

**Answer to Group Teaser 23**
Z belongs in Group 2. In Morse code, the letters in Group 1 all start with a dot. The letters in Group 2 all start with a dash. In Morse code, Z is "dash dash dot dot."

**Answer to Group Teaser 24**
The letters CDILMVX are all Roman numerals.

**Answer to Group Teaser 25**
They selected *Bianca Bubbles Buys a Balloon*. All of the names in this story, including Bianca, belong to the moons of Uranus. (They are also characters from Shakespearean plays.)

**Answer to Group Teaser 26**
Franklin. These are all of the first names that have been shared by multiple U.S. presidents (George Washington, H. W. Bush, and W. Bush; John Adams, Quincy Adams, Tyler, and Kennedy; James Madison and Monroe; Andrew Jackson and Johnson; William Harrison, McKinley, Taft, and Clinton; Franklin Pierce and D. Roosevelt).

**Answer to Group Teaser 27**
When you add the appropriate units, all of the values are equal to 1 metre: 39.37 inches, 3.281 feet, 1.0936 yards, and 0.00062 miles.

**Answer to Group Teaser 28**
These are the countries through which the 0 degree longitude line passes. The missing country is Togo, on the continent of Africa.

**Answer to Group Teaser 29**
BLEED does not belong. All the other words rhyme.

### Answer to Group Teaser 30

Each person likes a dessert with the same number of words as vowels in that person's name. "Shannon" has two vowels, so her favourite dessert is ice-cream. "Debbie" has three vowels, so her favourite dessert will have three words: strawberries and cream.

## Answers to Language Teasers

### Answer to Language Teaser 1

1. Mortimer was a tax collector.
2. Dirk was a lumberjack who died because he didn't hear his partner yell "Timber!"
3. Suzy was a comedian.
4. Ethel was a maid, always fighting dust.

### Answer to Language Teaser 2

My FATHER, the BATHER, would RATHER LATHER with soap than with body wash.

### Answer to Language Teaser 3

1. The cut on his HEEL won't HEAL in time for the race, so HE'LL have to drop out.
2. The man was so upset about being BALD that he regularly BALLED himself up on the bed and BAWLED his eyes out.
3. A pirate will wander the SEAS and essentially SEIZE everything he SEES.

### Answer to Language Teaser 4

1. Mite . . . Might
2. Sighted . . . Cited
3. Seer . . . Sear
4. Pail . . . Pale
5. Eye . . . Aye

### Answer to Language Teaser 5

1. Ponder . . . Yonder
2. Danger . . . Ranger
3. Towel . . . Vowel

### Answer to Language Teaser 6

1. Fighting a liar . . . Lighting a fire
2. Lack of pies . . . Pack of lies
3. Mad bunny . . . Bad money
4. Take a shower . . . Shake a tower
5. Shoving leopard . . . Loving shepherd

### Answer to Language Teaser 7

1. Grip gripe
2. Ant rant
3. Irate pirate
4. Latter platter
5. Thin thing

### Answer to Language Teaser 8

1. POLARISE (polar eyes)
2. AUTOBIOGRAPHY (auto biography)
3. COURTSHIP (court ship)
4. DILATE (die late)
5. LIABILITY (lie ability)

### Answer to Language Teaser 9

1. Bored . . . Board
2. Allowed . . . Aloud
3. Paced . . . Paste
4. Pleas . . . Please
5. Sachet . . . Sashay

### Answer to Language Teaser 10
1. under + stand = understand
2. short + cut = short cut
3. horse + shoe = horseshoe
4. tea + spoon = teaspoon
5. honey + moon = honeymoon

### Answer to Language Teaser 11
1. water + fall = waterfall
2. book + case = bookcase
3. star + fish = starfish
4. hair + dresser = hairdresser
5. butter + scotch = butterscotch

### Answer to Language Teaser 12
1. MELODRAMA (mellow drama)
2. PARLIAMENT (par lament)
3. OFFSPRING (off spring)
4. OVERBOARD (over board)

### Answer to Language Teaser 13
During the baseball game, the CHATTER didn't bother the LATTER BATTER, but it did bother the one before him.

### Answer to Language Teaser 14
1. Weeknight . . . Wee knight
2. Properties . . . Proper ties
3. Rapscallion . . . Rap scallion
4. Islander . . . I slander
5. Reincarnation . . . Rein carnation

### Answer to Language Teaser 15
1. Deer reed
2. Regal lager
3. Leg gel
4. Reel leer

### Answer to Language Teaser 16
The words, when combined with the correct placement letter, form new words.
a. Corn (acorn)
b. Leaf (belief)
c. Saw (see-saw)
d. Part (depart)
e. Mitt (emit)

### Answer to Language Teaser 17
1. The FUNCTION of a traffic light is to make a road JUNCTION safer.
2. Like the saying goes, you can't FORCE a HORSE to drink. He'll do it in due COURSE.
3. The JOCKEY was terrible at HOCKEY because he was much too short and kept slipping on the ice.

### Answer to Language Teaser 18
1. MANACLES
2. MANATEE
3. MANDATE
4. MANNEQUIN
5. MANUAL

### Answer to Language Teaser 19
1. DISADVANTAGE (staged)
2. SOMERSAULT (slates)
3. PENITENTIARY (pretty)
4. RETAINERS (strain)
5. SCARCITIES (access)

### Answer to Language Teaser 20
Each word can be changed into a new word by adding a letter of the alphabet to either the

beginning or the end. These new words fit the definitions.

1. Treaty (TREE-T)
2. Esquire (S-CHOIR)
3. Elfin (L-FIN)
4. Unite (U-KNIGHT)
5. Piccolo (PICKLE-O)
6. Entire (N-TIRE)

### Answer to Language Teaser 21
1. Trendy (TREND-E)
2. Extort (X-TORT)
3. Esteem (S-TEAM)
4. Embrace (M-BRACE)
5. Oboe (O-BOW)
6. Maybe (MAY-B)

### Answer to Language Teaser 22
Since you gained so much weight, your shoe doesn't fit any more. You must have TOO FAT A FOOT.

### Answer to Language Teaser 23
1. Intent
2. Inmate
3. Invent
4. Intern
5. Inspire

### Answer to Language Teaser 24
1. Assassin (S)
2. Fallible (L)
3. Pepper (P)
4. Assesses (S)
5. Minimum (M)

### Answer to Language Teaser 25
1. Russell the Leaf
2. Brad the Nail
3. Pattie the Hamburger
4. Sandy the Beach
5. Mark the Pen
6. Carrie the Basket

### Answer to Language Teaser 26
1. BEEF for a THIEF
2. A JESTER with a FESTER
3. Don't IMPEDE the STEED
4. A SHREW with a CLUE

### Answer to Language Teaser 27
1. Crimson . . . Red . . . Read . . . Perused (F)
2. Elk . . . Deer . . . Dear . . . Darling (D)
3. Pair . . . Two . . . Too . . . Also (E)
4. Soothsayer . . . Seer . . . Sear . . . Scorch (C)
5. Step . . . Stair . . . Stare . . . Gawk (B)
6. Quote . . . Cite . . . Site . . . Locale (A)

### Answer to Language Teaser 28
Cook before you sleep, from "Look before you leap."

### Answer to Language Teaser 29
1. Below elbow
2. Mentors monster
3. Hectare cheater
4. Alps pals
5. West stew

### Answer to Language Teaser 30
1. Gulp plug
2. Teaser eaters
3. Spam maps
4. Lease easel
5. Lotus louts

## Answers to Letter Equation Teasers

*Answer to Letter Equation Teaser 1*
12 = Months in a Year

*Answer to Letter Equation Teaser 2*
6 = Pockets on a Pool Table

*Answer to Letter Equation Teaser 3*
12 = Men on the Moon

*Answer to Letter Equation Teaser 4*
1 = Peck of Pickled Peppers that Peter Piper Picked

*Answer to Letter Equation Teaser 5*
13 = Cards in a Suit

*Answer to Letter Equation Teaser 6*
21 = Dots on a Die

*Answer to Letter Equation Teaser 7*
24 = Letters in the Greek Alphabet

*Answer to Letter Equation Teaser 8*
1,000 = Words a Picture is Worth

*Answer to Letter Equation Teaser 9*
26.2 = Miles in a Marathon

*Answer to Letter Equation Teaser 10*
5 = Rings on the Olympic Flag

*Answer to Letter Equation Teaser 11*
99 = Bottles of Beer on the Wall

*Answer to Letter Equation Teaser 12*
5 = Stars on the Chinese Flag

*Answer to Letter Equation Teaser 13*
100 = Zeros in a Googol

*Answer to Letter Equation Teaser 14*
60 = Miles Per Hour that a Cheetah can Run

*Answer to Letter Equation Teaser 15*
9 = Players on a Baseball Field

*Answer to Letter Equation Teaser 16*
2 = Turtle Doves and a Partridge in a Pear Tree

*Answer to Letter Equation Teaser 17*
88 = Keys on a Piano

*Answer to Letter Equation Teaser 18*
2 = Seats on a Tandem Bicycle

*Answer to Letter Equation Teaser 19*
3 = Little Kittens that Lost Their Mittens

*Answer to Letter Equation Teaser 20*
20 = Fingers and Toes on the Human Body

### Answer to Letter Equation Teaser 21

1 Chinese Lunar Year = 354 Days

### Answer to Letter Equation Teaser 22

9 = Squares in Noughts and Crosses

### Answer to Letter Equation Teaser 23

10 = Events in a Decathlon

### Answer to Letter Equation Teaser 24

3 = Primary Colours in the Colour Wheel

### Answer to Letter Equation Teaser 25

100 = Decades in a Millennium

### Answer to Letter Equation Teaser 26

23 = Pairs of Chromosomes in the Human Body

### Answer to Letter Equation Teaser 27

384,400 Kilometres = the Distance to the Moon from the Earth

### Answer to Letter Equation Teaser 28

2 = Legs in a Pair of Trousers

### Answer to Letter Equation Teaser 29

4 = Quarters in a Whole

## Answers to Logic Teasers

### Answer to Logic Teaser 1

From the second clue, we know that Cabin 5 is assigned to Miss D. Werk.

From the fourth clue, we know that Mr. Lastrain, Mr. Buss, and Mr. Meaner can only occupy cabin numbers 1, 2, and 3, although not particularly in that order. This leaves Miss Fortune and Mr. Allot with cabins 4 and 6, although not necessarily in that order.

From the third clue, we know that Mr. Buss (a smoker) must be in Cabin 3 and Mr. Allot (a nonsmoker), must be in Cabin 4. Thus, Miss Fortune is in Cabin 6.

From the fifth clue, we know that Mr. Meaner must be in Cabin 1, to give him the silence he needs during work. Hence, Mr. Lastrain is in Cabin 2.

Thus, the cabin numbers are:

1. Mr. Meaner
2. Mr. Lastrain
3. Mr. Buss
4. Mr. Allot
5. Miss D. Werk
6. Miss Fortune

### Answer to Logic Teaser 2

The combination was either VYWZXF or ZVFWXY. He only needs to try these two in order to rescue his puzzle collection. Solving this puzzle requires a method of trial and error. Start with the first combination and assume that one of the letters is in the correct position. Assuming the Y is correct, we know that the V in guess 2 is in the wrong position so it must be in the correct position in guess 3. Likewise W in guess 3 is wrong so its position in guess 2 must be correct. If W's position in guess 2 is correct, then F in guess 3 must be incorrect, which means its position in guess 2 is correct. Continue this logic until you arrive at the answer. (If your first assumption was incorrect you would arrive at an impossible situation and have to start over.)

### Answer to Logic Teaser 3

Bobby begins dropping readily available pebbles into the hole until the water level has risen enough for him to use the spoon. Sadly for Bobby, he never gets a doughnut.

### Answer to Logic Teaser 4

Bobby could draw a straight line from between 9 and 10 on the left side of the clock face to the right side between 3 and 4. The sum of the numbers on both sides of the line equals 39.

### Answer to Logic Teaser 5

The statement is "I always lie." If Bobby always lies, then that statement would be the truth, so he couldn't say it. If he always tells the truth, then he obviously couldn't say it because it would be a lie.

### Answer to Logic Teaser 6

The addresses are based on the first letters of the residents' relationship to me, converted to Roman numerals.

My Mother Vera = MMV = 2005
My Cousin Lucy = MCL = 1150

This leaves Me living at 1000 Neuron Street.

### Answer to Logic Teaser 7

1. Since a square is a type of rectangle, which is a type of parallelogram, which is a type of quadrilateral, then the comprehensive answer is (c), quadrilateral.

2. Since answers of (a), (b), or (c) would also result in (d) being correct, and an answer of (f) would result in (e) also being correct, the only possible answer is (e).

3. Since 7, 25, and anything greater than 9 are also greater than 6, neither (a), (c), nor (d) can be the answer because (b) would also be an answer. Therefore, the answer must be (b). (You can even take this one step further – assuming that only integers are used for numbering streets, the street number must be 8.)

### Answer to Logic Teaser 8

You should drink both vials. The answer cannot be determined from the clues, and if you think about it too long the poison will kill you. Even though you are sure to drink more poison, you are also sure to drink the antidote.

### Answer to Logic Teaser 9

You could make a circular chain with all the links using only three cuts and mends. Completely separate one of the four chains by cutting all three of its links. Use these three open links to connect the remaining three chains into a circle.

### Answer to Logic Teaser 10

In every game there is one loser. Since every person must lose once, except for the champ, there are 127 losers and therefore 127 games.

### Answer to Logic Teaser 11

There would be 4,950 handshakes. All 100 people at the fundraiser shake 99 hands. That's 9,900 when you multiply it, but two people participate in each handshake. Divide 9,900 by 2, and you have your answer.

### Answer to Logic Teaser 12

Four colours. In fact four colours will suffice for any map, real or fabricated. This famous theory was proposed in 1853, but it was not proved until 1977, when computers became available that could handle much of the number-crunching.

### Answer to Logic Teaser 13

If 12 chickens lay 24 eggs in four days, this means that each chicken lays two eggs, or one egg every two days. At this rate, it would take one chicken six days to lay three eggs.

### Answer to Logic Teaser 14

He can do it in one. Of the 10 barrels being shipped to the French fry factory, one contains heavy potatoes that weigh 1.1 pounds. Pete should take one potato from the first barrel, two from the second, three from the third, and so on until he has taken 10 potatoes from the last barrel. Then he should weigh all these potatoes together. His digital scale will give him a reading ending in a certain number of tenths of a pound. If the total weight ends in a .4, for instance, Pete will know that four of the potatoes are heavy. Since he knows that the only group of four potatoes came from the fourth barrel, he knows which barrel contains the heavy potatoes.

### Answer to Logic Teaser 15

The rook needs a minimum of 16 moves to pass over all the squares and return to the original position.

### Answer to Logic Teaser 16

From the first clue, we know Adam's last name and that he finished either first or second.

From the second clue, we know that Burch is neither Maggie nor Chris, which leaves who came in third. Maggie therefore came in fourth.

From the first clue, we can now see that Adam came in second and Chris came in first.

From the fifth clue, we know Boyle must be male and therefore Chris (making Maggie a Coriano).

From the third and fourth clues, we know that apple juice was third and therefore Jeff's. In summary:

Chris Boyle came in first with his water burp.

Adam Finn came in second with his soda burp.

Jeff Burch came in third with his apple-juice burp.

Maggie Coriano came in fourth with her milk burp.

### Answer to Logic Teaser 17

6,210,001,000 or 6,120,002,000.

Start with the letter A. It can only have values of 1,2, or 6 (we know this because we can count the letters). Assume that A=1. This creates an impossible situation for letter B, so it cannot be correct. Now, assume A=2. This creates an impossible situation for letter C. Therefore A=6. Similar reasoning can be used to arrive at the rest of the answers.

### Answer to Logic Teaser 18

Get three pieces of paper and put a unique mark on each of them.

Drop one in each chute and then go look in the skip. The piece of paper that is missing went into the outgoing mail. Put your rent cheque down that chute.

### Answer to Logic Teaser 19

The heaviest carriage goes first (11 tons) and crosses the bridge in 12 minutes. The engine returns (one minute) and takes the 5-ton carriage across in six minutes. It returns (one minute) and takes both the 5- and 2-ton carriages across (eight minutes). That's a total of 28 minutes.

### Answer to Logic Teaser 20

Green, Red, Blue, White, Yellow, Black

### Answer to Logic Teaser 21

From the fourth clue, we know that the cheeseburger had extra ketchup.

From the fifth clue, we know that the fish had mustard.

From the seventh clue, we know that the salad doesn't have mayo and that salad was not the first or last thing ordered. Combine these facts with the second clue, and we find that the salad had chilli sauce.

From the sixth clue, we know that Derek was third.

From the third clue, we know that Candy had chicken, and because of the first and fourth clues, we know she was second in line.

Therefore John was first in line, Rose was last, and Steve was fourth. The third and fifth now mean that neither Candy nor John had mustard; therefore, it must have been Steve. Since we know that the chicken was ordered second, the salad must have been ordered third by Derek, based on the first and seventh clues. This leaves Rose with the mayo hamburger. The only remaining option is for Candy to have ordered barbeque sauce and for John to have ketchup. In summary:

John was first in line and ordered a cheeseburger with extra ketchup.

Candy was second and ordered the chicken sandwich with barbeque sauce.

Derek was third and had a salad with chilli sauce.

Steve was fourth and ate a fish sandwich with mustard.

Rose was last in line and ate a hamburger with mayo.

### Answer to Logic Teaser 22
From the third clue, we know that the mango was either $4 or $5 and that Bobby purchased either four or five of them. But since the fourth clue tells us the $5 fruit was bought in twos, we know that he must have bought five $4 mangos. The fifth clue tells us that he bought five nectarines at $4. The sixth clue tells us that Bobby purchased two $5

pineapples, which means that there were four bananas, one orange, and three apples. From the sixth clue, we know that the bananas must have cost $1. In summary, Bobby purchased three apples at $3 each, one orange at $2, four bananas at $1, five nectarines at $4, and two pineapples at $5 each.

### Answer to Logic Teaser 23
Sue is the historian, Tina is the treasurer, Shannon is the president.

### Answer to Logic Teaser 24
Since the alien in the number 4 jersey doesn't have four limbs, it must have either two or three limbs. The three-limbed alien replies, so we know that number 4 cannot have three limbs. The alien who is number 4 must therefore have two limbs. This leaves number 2 with three limbs and number 3 with four limbs.

### Answer to Logic Teaser 25
Grandma should make apple-sauce or apple pie.

### Answer to Logic Teaser 26
From the first clue, we know that Bobby is the right fielder.

From the fourth clue, we know that Isaac is the catcher.

From the second clue, we know that the shortstop is female.

From the third clue, we know that Isabel got five runs as the shortstop.

From the first and third clues, we now know that Shane is the first baseman and Mimi is the pitcher. Going back to the third clue, we can now also solve for the remaining hits:

Bobby is the right fielder, and he got four hits.

Isaac is the catcher, and he got one hit.

Isabel is the shortstop, and she got five hits.

Mimi is the pitcher, and she got two hits.

Shane is the first baseman, and he got three hits.

### Answer to Logic Teaser 27
Go on Friday, when you can get everything done.

## Answers to Maths Teasers

### Answer to Maths Teaser 1
On a normal watch, the minute and hour hands should meet 11 times in 12 hours, at 12:00, 1:05, 2:11, 3:16, 4:22, 5:27, 6:33, 7:38, 8:44, 9:49, and 10:55. To work out how much time this leaves between each meeting of the hands, multiply 12 (the number of hours) by 60 (the number of minutes in an hour) and divide by 11 (the number of times the hands meet).$(12 \times 60) \div 11 = 65.45$ minutes, or 65 minutes and 27.27 seconds.

In Bobby's case, the hands meet after every 65 minutes, which

means the watch is gaining 27.27 seconds per hour.

### Answer to Maths Teaser 2
1,622,400. There are 52 possible letters (26 lower- and 26 upper-case) and 10 possible numbers. Per try, four characters can be selected, each try consisting of two letter characters and two number characters. These four characters can be arranged six different ways. (If @ is a letter and # is a number, these arrangements are ##@@, @@##, #@#@, @#@#, @##@, and #@@#.) Hence, the required answer is $52 \times 52 \times 10 \times 10 \times 6 = 1,622,400$ attempts.

### Answer to Maths Teaser 3
The club originally had 24 members. We can set up two equations, with two unknowns, which can easily be solved using algebra.

$$£3,120 = \text{Cost} \times \text{Members}$$
$$£3,120 =$$
$$(\text{Cost} + 26) \times (\text{Members} - 4)$$

### Answer to Maths Teaser 4
$$2.85 \times 1.60 \times 1.25 = 5.70$$
$$2.85 + 1.60 + 1.25 = 5.70$$

You can simplify this to 3 equations which can be solved using algebra. $A + B + C = 5.70$, $A \times B \times C = 5.7$, and $A + B + C = A \times B \times C$.

### Answer to Maths Teaser 5
Rod does. At the point Rod reaches the Puzzle Shop, Wally is only halfway there. By the time

Rod has run home again, Wally will have just made it to the shop.

### Answer to Maths Teaser 6

The box originally contained 27 doughnuts.

When Elmer finishes his third, the box contains just eight doughnuts, which means that when Smelly finished, he must have left 12 doughnuts. From this we can also tell that the remaining 12 doughnuts represented two-thirds of the amount left after Bobby finished. This tells us that Bobby must have left 18 doughnuts. We know that the box originally contained a third again more than that, which would equal nine more doughnuts. So there were originally 27 doughnuts in the box.

### Answer to Maths Teaser 7

520. There are 26 letters and 10 digits, for 260 possible combinations with the letter first and 260 more when the letter is last. That's a total of 520 possible horses.

### Answer to Maths Teaser 8

Hyde carried the heavy backpack 2 miles longer than Bobby did. It doesn't matter how long the actual hike was. On the way there, Hyde carried it for $x$ miles, and on the way home he carried it for 5 miles, for a total of $x + 5$ miles. Bobby carried it for 4 miles on the way there and for $x - 1$ miles on the way back (due

to the extra mile Hyde carried it) for a total of $x + 3$ miles. If you subtract $(x + 3)$ from $(x + 5)$ you get 2, which is the answer.

### Answer to Maths Teaser 9

Fold each corner into the centre of the cloth. This cuts the area in half (from 100 cm² to 50 cm²), and the robot will now accept the package.

### Answer to Maths Teaser 10

It broke at least 18 seconds ago. With 18 seconds between every doughnut, the age difference between the oldest and freshest is 144 seconds, so Old = Fresh + 144. We also know that Old = Fresh × 5. Plug the second equation into the first: Fresh × 5 = Fresh + 144, which solves to Fresh = 36. The age of the freshest doughnut is 36 seconds. Since the next doughnut was not produced on schedule 18 seconds later, the machine must have been broken for at least 18 seconds.

### Answer to Maths Teaser 11

The maximum amount that you can win is £671,088.64. One more doubling, and you will have gone over the £1 million maximum. This winning amount occurs between 12:26 and 12:27, so stop the clock then.

To arrive at the answer, start writing down the doublings starting with 1, 2, 4, 8, etc. (A calculator may help.) There are only 27 values below £1 million. Of these, only 3 of these have consecutive 8s. Pick the largest one.

### Answer to Maths Teaser 12

The ones digit will be 0. Both 2 and 5 are prime numbers. Anything multiplied by 2 and 5 will have a 0 in the ones place.

### Answer to Maths Teaser 13

There are 51 steps. The first thing the monk does is meditate on the middle step, which means the number of steps above him is equal to the number below. The easiest way to picture this is on a number line, with the middle step at 0. The monk's various rituals move his position up and down the number line like so: 0 + 8 − 12 + 1 + 2(14) = 25. This final value tells us how many steps the monk had to climb from the middle point to reach the top. Add the equal number that were below him, plus the middle step itself, for a total of 51.

### Answer to Maths Teaser 14

There are 6 contestants who ate a total of 42 bunnies.

From what the first contestant says, we know that Bunnies = 7 × Contestants. From the second contestant we know that 2 × (2/3)Bunnies = 10 × Contestants − 4. Just plug the first equation into the second equation and you can solve for Contestants, of which there are 6. Plug this back into

the first equation to determine that there are 42 bunnies.

### Answer to Maths Teaser 15

1.4 seconds. The squirrels can dig at speeds of 1/10th, 2/10ths, and 4/10ths of a hole per second, respectively. This means that if they work together, they can dig 7/10ths of a hole in one second, or 1.4 seconds for an entire hole.

### Answer to Maths Teaser 16

The watch must lose 24 hours total before it is back on correct time. Since it loses 6 minutes per hour, it will take 240 hours for it to lose 24 hours. 240 hours is exactly 10 days later at 8:00 P.M.

### Answer to Maths Teaser 17

Each ticket costs £32, and I bought 32 of them. If the number of tickets is the same as the ticket price, the total price is a perfect square. All we have to do is calculate the square root.

### Answer to Maths Teaser 18

36 pennies can make a square and triangle.

Write down the number of pennies that can make a triangle (3, 6, 10, 15, 21, 28, 36, etc.) and the number that can make a square (4, 9, 16, 25, 36, etc.). The first number both sets have in common is 36.

### Answer to Maths Teaser 19

987,652,413

The best way to solve this puzzle is by trial and error. Write down all the nine digit numbers you can think of until you find one that satisfies both conditions.

### Answer to Maths Teaser 20

Start the fast termite on the short stick and the slow termite on the long stick. When the fast termite has finished the short stick, 36 minutes will have elapsed (12 inches at 1 inch every three minutes). At this point, the long stick will have 7 inches remaining. If you put the fast termite at the other end of the remaining stick, the 7 inches will be eaten by both termites in 12 minutes – the slow termite will eat 3 inches and the fast termite will eat 4 inches. This totals 48 minutes.

### Answer to Maths Teaser 21

Start the slow termite on the longer stick. It will take the slow termite 16 minutes to eat 4 inches and make the sticks the same size. When the sticks are the same size, let the slow termite keep going, and start the fast termite on the other stick. This termite will finish his 12-inch stick in 36 minutes. That's 52 minutes elapsed so far, and the slow termite still has 3 inches left on his stick. Remove the slow termite, and let the fast termite

finish off the 3 inches in nine minutes for a total of 61 minutes.

### Answer to Maths Teaser 22

Going uphill for 10 miles, Bobby burns 0.286 gallons of gas. On the 5 miles of level land, Bobby burns 0.1 gallon each way. Going downhill the 10 miles back home, his car only consumes 0.125 gallons. That's a total of 0.611 gallons for the 30 mile trip. 30 divided by 0.611 is 49.1 mpg for the complete trip.

### Answer to Maths Teaser 23

26. Write down the two digit perfect squares and perfect cubes (it's a short list). It should be apparent from this list that 26 sits between 25 (a perfect square) and 27 (a perfect cube).

### Answer to Maths Teaser 24

I am 32 years old. The sum of all numbers 1 to x can be represented by the equation $x(x + 1)/2$. Since we know that this equation is equal to 528, we now have an easily solvable quadratic equation. Do you remember your algebra?

### Answer to Maths Teaser 25

The dog can run in a 6 foot radius circle.

To get the answer, first draw a right triangle. The long side (hypotenuse) is the length of the rope when fully stretched by the dog, 10 feet. The medium side is the distance from the ceiling to the dog's collar, 8 feet. The short side is the radius of the circle. Using the Pythagorean theorem, $a^2 + b^2 = c^2$, we get $a^2 + 8^2 = 10^2$ or $a = 6$.

### Answer to Maths Teaser 26

Because Santa started with trains, the 108th train will occur during his fifth batch of toys, for a total of 208. At 2 minutes a toy, he will complete his 108th train 416 minutes after he starts work, at 2:56 P.M.

### Answer to Maths Teaser 27

You can set up the following three equations and solve them to determine that Karin did the most press-ups, at 23.

$$T + K = 43$$
$$K + S = 41$$
$$S + T = 38$$

Solve the first and second equations so $T = 43 - K$ and $S = 41 - K$. Plug these into the third equation, and solve for K. Now plug this answer back into the first two equations to derive S and T.

### Answer to Maths Teaser 28

140 pogo sticks. The equation that defines this problem is $x + (x + 30) + (x + 60) + (x + 90) + (x + 120) = 1000$. Solve this equation to get $x = 140$.

### Answer to Maths Teaser 29

If you got 4, you are wrong. The correct answer is 6. Using the proper order of operations, you would do the division before you do the addition: $(4 \div 2) + 4 = 6$.

## Answers to Probability Teasers

### Answer to Probability Teaser 1

1. Since there are a million possible numbers, the odds of winning are 1:1,000,000.

2. Your odds of winning are 1:1,000,000 no matter what number you choose. This is true regardless of whether the number is the same as a previous winner or completely different.

3. Same answer as number 2.

4. In a single week, the odds are 1:1,000,000 that 50 will be chosen as the winner. To figure the odds for a two-week series, you multiply the odds for the first week by the odds for the second: 1:1,000,000 × 1:1,000,000 = 1:1,000,000,000,000, or one in a trillion.

5. Same answer as number 4. The odds are the same regardless of what two numbers are chosen for the two drawings. For each drawing, the odds are 1,000,000 that any number will be chosen. In a series of two drawings, the odds are one in a trillion that any two numbers will be chosen.

### Answer to Probability Teaser 2

The shower can be in six possible starting positions. The following possibilities could occur, with W standing for "wet" and D standing for "dry."

1. W, W, W, D, D, D
   (Player 1 loses)

2. W, W, D, D, D, W
   (Player 1 loses)

3. W, D, D, D, W, W
   (Player 1 loses)

4. D, W, W, W, D, D
   (Player 2 loses)

5. D, D, W, W, W, D
   (Player 1 loses)

6. D, D, D, W, W, W
   (Player 2 loses)

As you can see it's much better to be Player 2 – let your friend go first.

### Answer to Probability Teaser 3

Bobby should leave one pill in the blue jar and put all the others into the red jar. He has a 50 percent chance of choosing the blue jar, in which case he will definitely get a blue pill. If he chooses the red jar, filled half and half with red and blue pills, he still has nearly a 50 percent chance of picking a blue pill. Mathematically, his chances are .5 + .5(nearly .5) = nearly .75. All told, therefore, Bobby has nearly a 75 percent chance of getting a good blue pill.

### Answer to Probability Teaser 4

The last bird will be a baby duck. The only way a baby duck can be removed from the box is if you pick them in pairs. Since you started with an odd number of ducks, you will always have one left, which you will never be able to remove according to the rules.

### Answer to Probability Teaser 5

There is a 50 percent chance that the last person will sit in an assigned seat. The VIP will almost certainly sit in an already-assigned seat, and then everyone after him will sit in a random seat until someone sits in the one seat that has not been assigned, at which point everyone else will be able to sit in his or her own seat. The chances of the first person sitting in the unassigned seat are 1/200. The second person has 1/199 odds, and so on. If you sum these odds, you get 50 percent.

### Answer to Probability Teaser 6

Of the two coins, there are three sides that are heads. Two of the three times that you see a head, the other side will be head too, so the probability is 2/3.

### Answer to Probability Teaser 7

The odds are even. After the first person picks a number, the odds of the second person picking a different number as the first are 99/100. The odds of the third person picking an entirely different number are 98/100 and so on.

If you calculate the cumulative odds (by multiplying the individual odds for all 12 people), they are 50/100 (1 in 2, or 50 percent) when you reach the twelfth person.

### Answer to Probability Teaser 8

If the draughts board measures 12 inches on a side, its area is 144 square inches. If there are 8 squares to a side, for a total of 64, each square has an area of 144 ÷ 64 = 2.25 square inches. In other words, each square measures 1.5 inches wide by 1.5 inches high – .5 inches more than the diameter of the draughts piece. In order not to fall on a line, the centre of the draughts piece must fall within this "extra" 0.5 × 0.5 space inside each square. With 64 of these spaces, that gives us an area of 16 "safe" square inches out of the 144 square inches that make up the entire board. Thus, the odds are 16 in 144, or 1 in 9.

### Answer to Probability Teaser 9

The underground train heading south arrives at 0, 10, 20, 30, 40, and 50 minutes past the hour. The northbound train arrives at 2, 12, 22, 32, 42, and 52 minutes past the hour. This means there are only two minutes out of every ten when the next train will be the northbound train, but eight possible minutes when the next train will be going south. So if Bobby arrives at a random time, he will catch the southbound train four times as often as the other train.

### Answer to Probability Teaser 10

There are four possible ways for a mother to have two children: BB, BG, GB, GG. Since we know that both children cannot be girls, we have three remaining possibilities. Only one of these three arrangements includes two boys, so the probability of this is 1 in 3.

### Answer to Probability Teaser 11

Since there are 100 players, and everyone messes up with the same frequency, each and every player has a 1 percent chance of winning.

### Answer to Probability Teaser 12

There are 10 times in a day that have consecutive digits (1:23, 2:34, 3:45, 4:56, and 12:34, both A.M. and P.M.). In a day of 1440 minutes, the probability is 1 in 144.

### Answer to Probability Teaser 13

They each have the same 25-percent rate of making baskets.

### Answer to Probability Teaser 14

You should switch. Before the dime was shown, the average value of all three cups was 13.3 cents. Now that the dime has been removed from the equation, the average value of the two remaining cup is 15 cents, so you have a better chance of making more money by switching, on average.

**Answer to Probability Teaser 15**

It is very unlikely. There are 32 warts on the frog, and each wart can be one of three possible colours. This gives us $3^{32}$ different combinations, or 1,853,020,188,851,841. Only one of these combinations is "all purple," so the odds of this are 1 in 1,853,020,188,851,841.

**Answer to Probability Teaser 16**

This is tricky, because by holding a red marble you sacrifice the person to your left, but by holding a blue marble you sacrifice yourself. The game can only end when a red marble is selected. If everyone holds a red marble, only one person will be left. If only one person holds a red marble, it is possible for him to be the last person standing. The best solution is to alternate red and blue marbles down the entire line, starting and ending with red. This means that exactly four family members will be wearing dunce's caps, which guarantees that you will win.

**Answer to Probability Teaser 17**

Because the test is 95 percent reliable, if each person is tested 100 times, the liar will have a positive lie detector test 95 times. A truth teller will have five positive tests. Assume there are 100 people in Puzzleonia. Seven of them will be liars. Thus, if all 100 people are tested 100 times, the liars will produce 665 positive tests ($95 \times 7$) and the truth tellers will produce 465 positive tests ($93 \times 5$). The odds of the test being valid are $665 \div (665 + 465) = 59$ percent.

**Answer to Probability Teaser 18**

Zero. It's impossible for only three of the plants to be correctly labelled, since the fourth plant must therefore be correctly labelled as well.

**Answer to Probability Teaser 19**

Your child would have to eat an average of 5.5 meals to get all three toys. The average number of meals eaten to get the first toy is one. The odds of getting a new toy are 2 in 3 for any subsequent meal. This means that an average of 3/2 (1.5) meals will be eaten to get the second toy. The chances of getting the last toy once the first two have already been obtained are 1 in 3. Thus, the girl will need to eat an average of three meals in order to get the last toy. Add them all together and you will have the average number that the girl should expect to eat before collecting all three toys: 5.5 meals.

**Answer to Probability Teaser 20**

Since the centre sugar cube has no paint on it, the probability of all green faces pointing up is 0.

**Answer to Probability Teaser 21**

In order to finish in 15 minutes, he must use the short greeting on all 30 guests. Since the greeting length is random, the probability that all 30 greetings will be short is 1 in $3^{30}$, which is a rather large number: 1 in 205,891,132,094,649.

### Answer to Probability Teaser 22

There are $6 \times 6 \times 6 = 216$ possible outcomes of rolling 3 dice. You lose in the following cases: all dice are the same; two of the dice are the same; your roll is smaller than the other two; or your roll is bigger than the other two. There are only 40 outcomes in which you will win (8 if you roll a 2, 12 if you roll a 3, 12 if you roll a 4, and 8 if you roll a 5). This is a probability of 40/216, which is about 19 percent. Not very good odds.

### Answer to Probability Teaser 23

You are making two independent choices from 10 possible digits, which gives you 100 possible combinations. Since one of the two numbers must be greater than 5, that gives you four possibilities to work with: 9, 8, 7, and 6. From 9, you can subtract any of four numbers to leave a difference greater than 5: 0, 1, 2, or 3. From 8, you can subtract three numbers; from 7, you can subtract two; and from 6, you can subtract one. That makes 10 possibilities, and since the numbers can be in any order, you have 20 possible combinations out of 100 total, for a probability of 1 in 5.

### Answer to Probability Teaser 24

If there are only two people and two seats, they can sit in two possible ways. If there are three people and three seats, they can sit in four possible ways. Each person to sit down after the first one doubles the possibilities. Thus, 10 doublings will give you 1,024 possibilities ($2^{10}$).

### Answer to Probability Teaser 25

There are 500 rooms. Of these, 300 start with a 1, 2, or 3. Of those, only 90 end with a 4, 5, or 6. Therefore, the probability is 90 in 500, or 18 percent.

### Answer to Probability Teaser 26

For the 85 percent of times that a boy eats the last slice, the adult will think it's a girl 20 percent of the time. 20 percent of 85 percent is 17 percent. For the 15 percent of times that it is a girl, the adult will think it's a girl 80 percent of the time. 80 percent of 15 percent is 12 percent. That means that the adult will say that it is a girl $17 + 12 = 29$ percent of the time. The adult will be correct only 12 times out of 29. Thus, the probabilities are 12 in 29 that it was a girl and 17 in 29 that it was a boy.

### Answer to Probability Teaser 27

To get the total probability you simply multiply the individual probabilities. Thus the chances of having boy, boy, girl, girl is 52% $\times$ 52% $\times$ 48% $\times$ 48% = 6.2%. There are six ways to have two boys and two girls (bbgg, bgbg, bggb, ggbb, gbgb, gbbg), so the total probability is $6.2\% \times 6 = 37\%$.

**Answer to Probability Teaser 28**
The only way the same song can be played twice is if the last song of the first cycle is the same as the first song of the next cycle. There are 10 choices for the first song in the cycle, and one of those choices will be the previously played song. So, it will happen 10 percent of the time.

## Answers to Rebus Teasers

**Answer to Rebus Teaser 1**
Musical instruments

**Answer to Rebus Teaser 2**
Just between you and me.

**Answer to Rebus Teaser 3**
Abandon (a band on) ship. We're going down!

**Answer to Rebus Teaser 4**
Accentuate the positive.

**Answer to Rebus Teaser 5**
Watery grave. (The GRAVE has water ($H_2O$) in it.)

**Answer to Rebus Teaser 6**
*Last of the Mohicans*

**Answer to Rebus Teaser 7**
Backward glance

**Answer to Rebus Teaser 8**
Nothing between the ears

**Answer to Rebus Teaser 9**
Painless operation

**Answer to Rebus Teaser 10**
Long time no see (C).

**Answer to Rebus Teaser 11**
One step forward, two steps back.

**Answer to Rebus Teaser 12**
Making a monkey out of him

**Answer to Rebus Teaser 13**
Close, but no cigar.

**Answer to Rebus Teaser 14**
Put your money where your mouth is.

**Answer to Rebus Teaser 15**
What goes up must come down.

**Answer to Rebus Teaser 16**
I before E, except after C.

**Answer to Rebus Teaser 17**
Too close for comfort.

**Answer to Rebus Teaser 18**
Easy peasy (e's E, p's E)

**Answer to Rebus Teaser 19**
Wise guy

**Answer to Rebus Teaser 20**
Foreign currency (4 in cur in see)

**Answer to Rebus Teaser 21**
Forbidden fruit

**Answer to Rebus Teaser 22**
Up in smoke

**Answer to Rebus Teaser 23**
Forget about it.

**Answer to Rebus Teaser 24**
No two ways about it.

**Answer to Rebus Teaser 25**
In complete control

**Answer to Rebus Teaser 26**
Go out on a limb.

**Answer to Rebus Teaser 27**
A nervous breakdown

**Answer to Rebus Teaser 28**
You ought to be in pictures.

**Answer to Rebus Teaser 29**
Tennessee

## Answers to Riddle Teasers

**Answer to Riddle Teaser 1**
A television remote control, often used by a "couch potato." Channels are most often changed between programs, which end on the hour or half-hour. If you lose the batteries, the only way to control the television is by hand.

**Answer to Riddle Teaser 2**
A grand piano. The "closest friends" are the strings, which are tightly strung.

**Answer to Riddle Teaser 3**
Horses. You can be "hungry as a horse," and power is measured in horsepower. The second line refers to the Four Horsemen (and therefore four horses) of the Apocalypse. Some people "gain wealth" when they win money betting on horse races. Wild horses are said to be "broken" when they are tamed.

**Answer to Riddle Teaser 4**
Fish. The riddle refers to the phrases "Drink like a fish" (which will cause you to have to excuse yourself) and "Sleep with the fishes" (meaning you're dead).

**Answer to Riddle Teaser 5**
An ostrich. "Brothers" is referring to other types of birds.

**Answer to Riddle Teaser 6**
Jupiter. As a planet, it is a gas giant, and it has the Great Red Spot (which looks like an eye) on its surface. As a god, Jupiter was the king of gods in Roman mythology, and he wielded a lightning bolt.

**Answer to Riddle Teaser 7**
Pi. Most people know the first few digits, but do not know the last (since pi never ends).
It sounds like "pie" but isn't. The Greek symbol for pi is made up of three wavy lines.
If you know the straight-line distance (here to there), pi will

help you calculate the distance around a circle.

### Answer to Riddle Teaser 8

A computer mouse pad. A computer mouse (rodent) "walks" over a mouse pad. A mouse pad's job is to just lie there. Mouse pads aren't as useful since the invention of the optical mouse.

### Answer to Riddle Teaser 9

The woman from Troy had a camera and the woman from Dreck had an Etch-a-Sketch. A camera takes in light (eats up sunshine) to create a picture, which can be thought of as "remembering" the picture's subject. You twist and turn the knobs of an Etch-a-Sketch to make a picture (possibly of an urn), and erase the picture by flipping ("upending") the unit.

### Answer to Riddle Teaser 10

The Statue of Liberty. The statue welcomes immigrants to the United States. It travelled in pieces across the Atlantic Ocean from France. The colour of the copper statue changed from brownish to green because of oxidation, the effect of oxygen on the copper.

### Answer to Riddle Teaser 11

A wedding ring. It is worth more as a symbol to its owner than its actual monetary worth. It symbolizes the start of a marriage,

and its circular shape implies no end. It reminds you of your spouse, who is your "true, dear friend."

### Answer to Riddle Teaser 12

Dirt. All life on Earth depends on the soil, either directly or indirectly, but it is very cheap to buy ("dirt cheap," in fact). The number of stars has been compared to the number of grains of sand on the beaches. People who are treated badly are said to be treated "like dirt."

### Answer to Riddle Teaser 13

An automobile tyre. A tyre is like a sneaker to a car. If a tyre is run through it goes flat and the car "comes up lame." The tyres will move the car in any direction. Cars are often repaired on a lift, where the tyres get a "rest."

### Answer to Riddle Teaser 14

They are the seven levels of classification used in categorizing living things: Kingdom (like a monarchy), Phylum (no clue given), Class (where you go to learn), Order (the opposite of a mess), Family (like mum, dad, etc.), Genus ("genius" minus an "i"), Species (like the human species – you and me).

The last verse simply gives a hint in the word "mammal," which is a class designator.

### Answer to Riddle Teaser 15

The Olympic rings. The rings are interlocked (holding hands). They are known throughout the world. The emotions listed are associated with colours, which the last verse implies when it says that you should be thinking of rainbows: mournful, blue; evil, black; mad, red; fearful, yellow; jealous, green (with envy). These, in order, are the five colours of the Olympic rings. The land of Zeus is Greece, where the first Olympics were held. The rings are normally on a white flag ("wintry sail"). The location of the Olympics is voted on by the Olympic committee.

### Answer to Riddle Teaser 16

A mirror. A mirror seems to reverse right and left, but it doesn't actually do that.
The mirror "sees" you when you look at it.

### Answer to Riddle Teaser 17

An elephant. The riddle refers to the elephant's trunk, the loud noise an elephant makes, the fact that it needs to eat, and the bad smell.

### Answer to Riddle Teaser 18

Tarot cards. Tarot cards are used to predict the future. The dimensions of the cards are that of a neat (trig) rectangle. Four cards are the Hanged Man, the Devil, Stars, and Death.

### Answer to Riddle Teaser 19

The letter Z. To some it's pronounced "zee," and to some it's pronounced "zed." "Confused" has a "z" sound in it, but an "s" is used instead.

### Answer to Riddle Teaser 20

The act of card shuffling. The picture cards (royalty) are mixed with the other cards (masses). A trickster can easily control the top and bottom (border) cards while shuffling. Since most games end with like cards grouped together, shuffling is used to separate these cards "that are the same."

### Answer to Riddle Teaser 21

A toothbrush. A toothbrush glides over teeth (hills and valleys), cleaning away food and bacteria (vile things). The person commanding the toothbrush is the one who ate the food in the first place. A full set of human teeth contains 32 teeth (meta "four" $\times 8 = 32$).

### Answer to Riddle Teaser 22

A skeleton. Skeletons support our bodies, but are considered by many to be scary. There are 206 bones in a human skeleton: 10 score (200), plus a handful (5), plus another by your beard (the jawbone) equals 206.

### Answer to Riddle Teaser 23

The *Star Wars* movies. The order of release was Episodes 4, 5, 6,

1, 2, and so on. The Jedi religion is prevalent in all of the movies. The stories seem futuristic, but actually took place "A long time ago . . . " The first *Star Wars* movie (Episode 4) was released in 1977.

**Answer to Riddle Teaser 24**
Paper. "Great" trees are used to make paper. Trees are the largest living things on the planet and are therefore our grandest kin. A "sea of paperwork" is a common phrase. With the development of the computer chip we were promised a "paperless society," which has not developed.

**Answer to Riddle Teaser 25**
The man from Poland Springs has some pencils, and the man from Duff has pens. At the will of the user, a pencil can erase what it was used to create, usually leaving a faint shadow behind. Pens use liquid ("juices") instead of graphite and are generally neater than pencils. The average pen is useless in a zero-gravity environment because the ink won't flow. Pencils, however work fine.

**Answer to Riddle Teaser 26**
Even numbers. When you add even numbers, the answer stays even. When you add odd numbers, the odds are changed ("perverted") to evens. When you add odds and evens, the answer is always odd (and therefore the evens "lose"). Negative numbers raised to an even power result in a positive answer. The noontide hour is an even number. Most things are grouped in even numbers, except for weekdays – adding one day would make eight.

**Answer to Riddle Teaser 27**
A refrigerator. Except for heating devices, heat generally indicates an inefficiency in machines. Refrigerators (and freezers) generate heat by removing it from their insides. Therefore, a hot exterior indicates that the unit is working efficiently. Refrigerators can be considered "feeders" because they indirectly provide food. A refrigerator's job is to reduce heat.

**Answer to Riddle Teaser 28**
A game die. Numbers on opposite sides of a die add up to seven. All of the numbers on one die add up to 21. A standard die has six sides. Dice are used for simple games or high-stakes gambling. You must throw them to use them.

## Answers to Science Teasers

**Answer to Science Teaser 1**
He should raise his sails, since he can then tack into the wind. The apparent wind to the pirate is a 3-knot head-wind since he is travelling with the current. Tacking is a

way that a sailor can arrange the sails to sail almost directly into the wind. He could zig-zag down the river slightly faster than the current by using this technique. Hopefully those chasing him aren't so clever.

### Answer to Science Teaser 2

Bobby should choose to stay for one year. On Venus, a year (one full orbit around the Sun) is 224.7 Earth days, and a day (a full rotation of the planet) is 243 Earth days. This means that a day is longer than a year on Venus!

### Answer to Science Teaser 3

First, place one end of the little piece of string on top of the ice. Second, sprinkle some salt on the ice. The salt will cause the ice to melt and refreeze around the string. Now you can lift out the cube and win your free lunch.

### Answer to Science Teaser 4

Fire. If you light the bottom of a rope, it will quickly climb the rope. If you light the top of the rope, it will take some time for it to reach the bottom. Ever wondered why a candle will burn for so long? (Of course the wax also helps.)

### Answer to Science Teaser 5

You should choose the three thin blankets. This is because air acts as an insulator, so the layer of air captured between the thin blan-

kets will increase the total insulation and keep you warmer.

### Answer to Science Teaser 6

The cable will be stronger because as a material is made into smaller and smaller fibres, the chance for defects causing a major failure decreases. Think of it this way: Cut a quarter of the way through the rod, and do the same to the cable. With the cable, three quarters of the wires will still be in perfect condition. The rod, however has a large crack in it now, and it is very easy to break something when there is already a crack started.

### Answer to Science Teaser 7

In the movies you almost always hear the sounds of objects exploding or spaceships firing lasers. Since sound can't travel in a vacuum, including outer space, this is impossible.

### Answer to Science Teaser 8

When liquids are mixed, the molecules can arrange themselves so that they fit together more tightly than either of the original, pure liquids. A good way to visualize this is to picture a box completely filled with billiard balls (representing large molecules). If you pour sand (representing small molecules) into the box, the sand will fill the voids between the billiard balls. The mass in the box will increase, but the total volume will not change. Jimmy can prove his innocence by weighing the mixture. His combination of liquids will equal the original weight of the water plus the weight of the ethanol.

### Answer to Science Teaser 9

The balloon will sink. At a depth of 60 feet, the water pressure is greater than it is at 30 feet (by about 15 psi). Because of this, the balloon will shrink, causing the balloon/weight system to increase in density (the total volume will become smaller while the total mass stays the same). Since the system is now more dense than it was at 30 feet, it will sink. Also important is the fact that since water is pretty much incompressible, the water density at both depths will be about the same.

### Answer to Science Teaser 10

Heat. "Powdered water" is of course finely crushed ice, and to get what you really want (liquid water), you only need to add heat.

### Answer to Science Teaser 11

Since the moon has no atmosphere, it is already under vacuum. The reason a vacuum cleaner works is that the pressure drop between the air in the room and the vacuum bag causes air to rush into the bag, carrying dust and dirt with it. Since there is no

pressure drop between the vacuum chamber and the moon's surface, you could not suck up moon dust with a vacuum cleaner.

### Answer to Science Teaser 12

He can boil the water by applying a vacuum to the container. Boiling occurs when the molecules in a liquid begin to fly about independently – typically heat is added to give the particles more energy, but changes in pressure will also affect them. Once the pressure is low enough, it will no longer hold the molecules in place. So as the pressure drops, the boiling point will also drop. The water will eventually boil without gaining any heat – it will remain at room temperature. The scientist can then quickly relieve the vacuum and pour the water over his head without worry of scalding himself.

### Answer to Science Teaser 13

The third unit, which analyzed the contents of the chamber, is definitely a fake. "Air" is a name that we give to the combination of gases that make up our atmosphere. It is made up of oxygen, nitrogen, carbon dioxide, and trace amounts of several other chemicals. Because of this, there is no such thing as one molecule of air. If there really is only one molecule in the chamber, it would be a molecule of oxygen, nitrogen, or one of the other chemicals. A piece of analysis equipment would never call it "air."

### Answer to Science Teaser 14

The only reason that the scientist could see the assistant's hand is that light from the sun reflected off the hand and travelled to the scientist's eye. This light that allowed him to see the hand travels at the same speed as the light from the torch. If light travelled slowly, the scientist would still see the hand go up at the same time as he saw the light get turned on. He would just see both things happen a few seconds after they actually happened.

### Answer to Science Teaser 15

Because of water tension, the water at the edge of a glass will climb slightly up the inner sides. This means that the water level rises at the edges. Since ice cubes float, they will float to the highest point, which is at the edges. However, the water tension will allow you to overfill a glass just above the rim, and then the highest point will be in the centre of the glass. Try it sometime.

### Answer to Science Teaser 16

A tight-rope walker remains standing by keeping his centre of mass directly above the rope. If his centre of mass moves off centre, he must either correct

this or rotate off the rope and fall down. The balancing poles are frequently droopy and weighted at the tips. This lowers the centre of mass of the performer, which also makes it easier to balance. Also, by carrying a long pole, the performer is increasing his rotational inertia. This means that he will rotate slower and therefore have more time to make a correction to his centre of mass.

### Answer to Science Teaser 17

The balloon will actually move to the right. This is because the balloon always moves in the direction opposite to gravity. When the car is turning right, the apparent gravity is away from the centre of the turn. This is why Bobby falls to the left. The balloon does the opposite.

### Answer to Science Teaser 18

Dan suffocated because the air that he exhaled up the pipe could not travel far enough before he inhaled it back in. In other words, the volume inside the hollow walking stick was greater than the volume of Dan's lungs. Eventually he was just breathing carbon dioxide and he passed out. Don't try this at home.

### Answer to Science Teaser 19

The rope is not rigid, so at any point you could pull the rope up and you would have 3 extra feet of rope. If the rope was rigid and floated an equal distance above all points of the earth, you would have a gap of almost 6 inches! (To calculate this, use the equation C = 2πr, where C = 24,901.55. Notice that adding 3 feet to C increases r by about 6 inches.)

### Answer to Science Teaser 20

Find the container with mercury. Pour the mercury into the tube. Since steel is lighter than mercury, the ball will float to the top and you can easily grab it.

### Answer to Science Teaser 21

The beer mug is more likely to crack. Because glass is a poor heat conductor, the heat will pass through the thick beer glass slowly. This will cause the glass to expand unevenly and have a much higher chance of cracking.

### Answer to Science Teaser 22

Nothing would happen. Fire needs oxygen to burn, and there is no oxygen in the sealed room.

### Answer to Science Teaser 23

Bobby took his bird onto an airplane, where it got loose and flew to the front of the cabin at 10 mph. Thus, it was travelling at a total of 410 mph.

### Answer to Science Teaser 24

79 psi. Pressure gauges are set to read at 0 when the pressure being measured is the same as atmospheric pressure. True 0 psi only occurs in a complete vacuum. Since atmospheric pressure

is about 15 psi, then the real pressure of the original tyre is 32 + 15 = 47 psi. You can now double it to get 94 psi. Accounting again for atmospheric pressure, the gauge will read 94 – 15 = 79 psi.

### Answer to Science Teaser 25

The hollow Jawbreaker has its mass distributed around its edge, while the solid Jawbreakers have their mass distributed evenly. As a result, the solid Jawbreakers will accelerate quicker when rolled or spun. Simply spin or roll some Jawbreakers on a flat surface and take the slowest one.

### Answer to Science Teaser 26

No. A refrigerator needs to do something with all that heat it's sucking out of the inside of the fridge. It usually pumps it out the back. As far as the kitchen is concerned, there is no change in temperature in the long run. When you first open the door, the temperature may drop a little bit, but because of the heat coming out of the back of the refrigerator, once everything equalizes, the temperature of the room will stabilise.

### Answer to Science Teaser 27

The smaller balloon is exerting a greater force on the air inside. (This is why it's hardest to blow up a balloon at the beginning and easier once it's already got some air in it.) Because of this greater force, the small balloon will push all its air into the large balloon.

### Answer to Science Teaser 28

If you put a raisin into a glass of soda it will sink. Then, little bubbles will stick to it until it has enough to float to the surface. Once it hits the surface, the bubbles will pop and the raisin will sink again. This will happen until the carbonation runs out or you eat the raisin.

## Answers to Series Teasers

### Answer to Series Teaser 1

9 would go between 4 and 1, and 10 would go between 6 and 3. They are arranged alphabetically, according to the written numbers.

### Answer to Series Teaser 2

The final letter should be D. The series was created from the phrase "A penny saved is a penny earned" by removing the spaces and reversing groups of three letters at a time.

### Answer to Series Teaser 3

If you place the first few letters in the alphabet in front of these words you will get new words: A-BASH, B-ALE, C-ABLE, D-EAR, E-BONY.

### Answer to Series Teaser 4

K. These are the periodic elements with single letter symbols.

Potassium (K) is the next element with a one-letter symbol.

### Answer to Series Teaser 5

These are the first letters of the Greek alphabet (alpha, beta, gamma, delta, epsilon, zeta, eta, theta). The next Greek letter is iota, so the next letter is I.

### Answer to Series Teaser 6

The next number (and the next, and the next) is 9. Each number is the sum of the digits in the previous number.

### Answer to Series Teaser 7

Grover. These are the first names of U.S. presidents, listed alphabetically by last name.

### Answer to Series Teaser 8

These are the biggest countries of the world listed in decreasing land area.

### Answer to Series Teaser 9

These are the times when the hour and minute hand overlap, and are all an hour and five minutes apart. The next time is 9:49.

### Answer to Series Teaser 10

22. These are the numbers that start with the letter T.

### Answer to Series Teaser 11

Ea. These are the first two letters of the planets' names. The missing planet is Earth.

### Answer to Series Teaser 12

Ant-eater. The first letter in each animal's name is a consecutive letter of the alphabet. Based on this pattern, the first animal must start with A.

### Answer to Series Teaser 13

These are the chess pieces in the back row for the white player. (Rook, knight, bishop, queen, king, bishop, knight, rook.)

### Answer to Series Teaser 14

The missing symbol is %, and it goes between $ and ^. These are the symbols going from left to right on the numbered keys of a keyboard.

### Answer to Series Teaser 15

D. Each three-letter group is its own word: THE, HER, ERA, RAT, ATE, and TEN. To make "en" a word, add D and get END.

### Answer to Series Teaser 16

South. The first letters of each word are the musical scale (doh re mi fa soh lah ti doh). The missing word must start with "so."

### Answer to Series Teaser 17

317. Each number is the previous number doubled, plus 3.

### Answer to Series Teaser 18

Heaven. Each word rhymes with its order in the list (one = run, two = glue, and so on).

### Answer to Series Teaser 19

"Love" and "Game." This series shows consecutive scores for a game of tennis.

### Answer to Series Teaser 20

He stopped at the sweet factory. Each location has one more syllable than the previous location. "Sweet factory" is five syllables long, so it was the fifth place he stopped.

### Answer to Series Teaser 21

Quickly. Once this final word is added, the sentence contains every letter in the alphabet.

### Answer to Series Teaser 22

31 and 37. This is a list of prime numbers.

### Answer to Series Teaser 23

This is a series of national capitals, listed alphabetically by country.

### Answer to Series Teaser 24

These are the letters in the Hawaiian alphabet. The missing letter is W.

### Answer to Series Teaser 25

These are the digits of pi after the decimal point. After 1415926535, the next few digits are 897932.

### Answer to Series Teaser 26

S. These are the first letters of the words in the teaser.

## Answers to Situational Teasers

### Answer to Situational Teaser 1
The stranger was a newborn baby. His wife had gone into labour, hence the telephone call while he was at work. The neighbour had called Bobby to inform him.

### Answer to Situational Teaser 2
The real time is 10:35.
To solve this, simply draw a standard clock on a sheet of thin paper, with the time showing as 7:55. Now flip the paper over, left to right (as if you were turning the page of a book). This simulates looking in a mirror. Then rotate the paper 180 degrees to simulate the clock being upside down. Hold the paper up to the light, and the time will show as 10:35.

### Answer to Situational Teaser 3
Simply pile up all of the books except the one that measures 1 inch. This will give you 18 inches. Open the top book, and turn enough pages to measure 1 inch. Use the yardstick to verify the height. (If you want to be really accurate, you should actually open the bottom book, because then the other books will flatten the bulge the open book makes.)

### Answer to Situational Teaser 4
The boy threw the tennis ball straight up.

### Answer to Situational Teaser 5
The tree had been growing like a normal tree above the water. Then a dam was built and the entire valley was flooded to make an artificial lake. The tree was now under water, but it didn't live long.

### Answer to Situational Teaser 6
Robby is a fireman. The water from his hose damaged some paintings as he put out a fire in the gallery, but in the process he rescued hundreds of millions of dollars' worth of other artwork.

### Answer to Situational Teaser 7
If he lets some air out of his tyres, his lorry will get a little shorter, and he can get un-stuck.

### Answer to Situational Teaser 8
Bobby takes one nut from each of the remaining tyres and uses them together on the spare. This gives him three nuts for each tyre, which is enough to get him to the nearest mechanic.

### Answer to Situational Teaser 9
The piece of paper was the race-card, where all the horses' names are listed. It had the name of the winning horse as well as the nine losing horses' names.

### Answer to Situational Teaser 10
The bank robber did not rob the bank this time. He was just withdrawing money from his account.

Nothing illegal happened, so the officer didn't do anything.

### Answer to Situational Teaser 11

Pick up a sugar cube.

### Answer to Situational Teaser 12

Put a few ice-cubes from your water glass into the coffee and let them melt. When your new cup of coffee comes, you can test the temperature. If it is cold, the waiter just removed the fly and served you the same coffee. Now you know not to tip him.

### Answer to Situational Teaser 13

The directions at the top of the test told the students to do nothing.

### Answer to Situational Teaser 14

The man heard his floorboards squeak in a familiar way and knew that a robber was in his house. He called the police, who came and arrested the robber.

### Answer to Situational Teaser 15

The man dropped the 1,000 feet by taking the lift from the top of the Empire State building to the ground.

### Answer to Situational Teaser 16

He had gone to the beach the previous day, so he was already sunburned when he went outside to get the paper.

### Answer to Situational Teaser 17

It was a horse race – the horse's owner got all the money, not the horse itself.

### Answer to Situational Teaser 18

The gunshot was on the television in the other room.

### Answer to Situational Teaser 19

One of the cars was a hearse that was carrying a coffin. The man inside was already dead.

### Answer to Situational Teaser 20

Inspector Bobby Braingle noticed that the feet of the woman were three feet from the floor, but he could see that the seat of the chair would only be two feet high when it was upright. It would have been impossible for the woman to stand on the chair and put the rope around her neck, hence someone must have held her up. The chair was then put there to make it look like suicide.

### Answer to Situational Teaser 21

The man had been buried in the sand so he couldn't get up (even though he really wanted to).

### Answer to Situational Teaser 22

The man is a physics teacher and is demonstrating the law of energy conservation by tying the brick to a string hanging from the ceiling. He pulls the brick back and puts it right up to his nose and lets go. Because of air friction, the brick should lose some speed and thus miss the teacher's nose on the return swing. Unfortunately, this time the teacher accidentally gives the brick a little push. It returns with too much force and breaks his nose.

### Answer to Situational Teaser 23

Hank and Wanda are fish. Their fish bowl was knocked off the table by an earthquake.

### Answer to Situational Teaser 24

A snowman was standing there before it melted.

### Answer to Situational Teaser 25

They hired a photographer to take some photos.

### Answer to Situational Teaser 26

The man was an astronaut. When he took off his pressurised hat (helmet), he suffocated.

### Answer to Situational Teaser 27

Friday mornings are street-cleaning days on Bobby's street, so if he parked there on Thursday night, his car would get towed.

### Answer to Situational Teaser 28

The man is a cartoon character. When the piano landed on his head, he saw stars for a few seconds but was then okay.

## Answers to Trick Teasers

### Answer to Trick Teaser 1

Bobby and his motorcar were on the train – he as a passenger and the car as freight.

### Answer to Trick Teaser 2

A ton is a ton regardless of what it is measuring. There are a lot more cotton balls in a ton than there are gold bricks, but a ton of each would weigh the same.

### Answer to Trick Teaser 3

The amount of water in the glass will be the same regardless of whether the ice is frozen or melted. Ice is still water, it's just frozen.

### Answer to Trick Teaser 4

Stop imagining.

### Answer to Trick Teaser 5

If you cut "8" right down the middle, you have 3.

### Answer to Trick Teaser 6

"Beam me up, Scotty."

### Answer to Trick Teaser 7

M and Y

### Answer to Trick Teaser 8

Use the toothpicks to form the number 4. The top part contains a triangle, and the number 4 is a perfect square ($2 \times 2 = 4$).

*Answer to Trick Teaser 9*
Using Roman numerals, 11 is XI.
Cut this in half horizontally and
you have VI, or 6.

*Answer to Trick Teaser 10*
Since the airplane isn't crashing,
they will all live.

*Answer to Trick Teaser 11*
Jane could purchase all three
things, or anything else worth
£111. She took with her an
Alexander Hamilton (£10), a Ben
Franklin (£100), and a George
Washington (£1).

*Answer to Trick Teaser 12*
The letter S (seven – S = even).

*Answer to Trick Teaser 13*
Two are left. The monkey who
climbed down was named "Two."

*Answer to Trick Teaser 14*
Bobby said, "I am ready to go."
Bobby wasn't in jail – his
lawyer was.

*Answer to Trick Teaser 15*
12:55 because it's "5 to 1." At
12:50, it's only "10 to 1."

*Answer to Trick Teaser 16*
Amber is the only girl, so she
goes to the girls' locker room.
The three boys go to the boys'
locker room.

*Answer to Trick Teaser 17*
July 4 is Keiko's birthday.

*Answer to Trick Teaser 18*
You have £300 left, since you
took the apples. You really
should have paid for them.

*Answer to Trick Teaser 19*
Zero. There is sure to be someone in Australia who has no toes
on one foot. Anything multiplied
by zero is zero.

*Answer to Trick Teaser 20*
This time they were playing tennis, not poker. An ace is a winning serve, which Phyllis did on
match point to win the game.

*Answer to Trick Teaser 21*
A baseball team. The nine people have a total of 18 feet.

*Answer to Trick Teaser 22*
The sheep will never eat all of
the grass because it grows faster
than they can eat it.

*Answer to Trick Teaser 23*
Bobby has an Apple computer,
not the fruit.

*Answer to Trick Teaser 24*
These are just ordinary quarters,
but 1,976 of them makes £494.

*Answer to Trick Teaser 25*
Bobby draws a picture. Everyone
knows that a picture is worth
1,000 words.

*Answer to Trick Teaser 26*
He saw a group of crows, which
is called a "murder."

### Answer to Trick Teaser 27

Unlock the door and get out.

### Answer to Trick Teaser 28

The teaser told you the answer: "What" doesn't belong.

### Answer to Trick Teaser 29

All animals drink with their eyes. They can't just take them out of their eye sockets.

## Answers to Trivia Teasers

### Answer to Trivia Teaser 1

When Queen Elizabeth was born on April 21, 1926, no one could have possibly known she would have been the heir to the throne. Her father wasn't crowned king until his brother, King Edward VIII, abdicated some 10 years later.

### Answer to Trivia Teaser 2

1. "I Saw Her Standing There"
2. "Lucy in the Sky with Diamonds"
3. "Day Tripper"

### Answer to Trivia Teaser 3

Hamate. These are the bones in your hand, not including the fingers.

### Answer to Trivia Teaser 4

Alligators only live in the southeastern United States. Crocodiles live in the Amazon.

### Answer to Trivia Teaser 5

In a blackjack game. In blackjack, the ace can represent 11 or 1. In this case, although the ace started out being worth 11, it is now counted as 1 to keep the total from going over 21.

### Answer to Trivia Teaser 6

1. A group of buzzards is a wake.
2. A group of cobras is a quiver.
3. A group of turtles is a bale.
4. A group of sharks is a shiver.

### Answer to Trivia Teaser 7

There were only four people in existence when Cain killed his brother Abel (Adam, Eve, Cain, and Abel). This is recorded in the Bible and many Bible story books.

### Answer to Trivia Teaser 8

The two letters are Q and O, for Qatar and Oman.

### Answer to Trivia Teaser 9

4332. These are the number of days that it takes each planet to orbit the sun, starting with Mercury. The next planet is Jupiter, which orbits every 4,332 days.

### Answer to Trivia Teaser 10

In official golf rules, you are allowed to lift your ball to determine if it's yours, but you can only do this if your ball is not in a hazard. Since Bobby's ball is in a hazard, he is not allowed to touch it. Fortunately, another rule states that there is no penalty for playing the wrong ball from a hazard. Bobby should pick one ball and play it. If he then finds out it's not his, he can play the other ball.

**Answer to Trivia Teaser 11**
Stephen Hawking was only 13 when Albert Einstein died, so this meeting could have never taken place.

**Answer to Trivia Teaser 12**
It wasn't until 1969 that women could be declared "incorrigible." Thus, no women could ever have been sent to Alcatraz.

**Answer to Trivia Teaser 13**
Christmas in the southern hemisphere occurs in the summer; therefore, he couldn't have been building a snowman.

**Answer to Trivia Teaser 14**
Kalliope. These are the nine muses from Greek mythology.

**Answer to Trivia Teaser 15**
Azerbaijan and Afghanistan

**Answer to Trivia Teaser 16**
If he pours boiling fluid on a frozen pane of glass, the rapid expansion will cause it to shatter.

**Answer to Trivia Teaser 17**
Phytoplankton floats around in the ocean and is not rooted in place.

**Answer to Trivia Teaser 18**
The total must add up to 100 percent, so the missing term is 3.7 percent. These numbers represent the percent of total land area for each continent on Earth (Asia, Africa, North America, South America, Antarctica, Europe, Australia). The missing 3.7 percent accounts for all the islands not included in any continent.

**Answer to Trivia Teaser 19**
The doctor told Bobby to buy some blinds and stop scheduling his sleep around the sun. Bobby lives in Alaska, and it is nearing the end of spring. The days are getting longer and longer, which means that the nights are getting shorter and shorter. Since Bobby sleeps only when it is dark, he is getting less and less sleep each night. (Where Bobby lives, the shortest night has only three hours of darkness, so he will be getting very little sleep if he doesn't do something.)

**Answer to Trivia Teaser 20**
The "thumbs up" signal in scuba diving means that the person wants to surface, so Bobby and Nobby go up and get some fresh air.

**Answer to Trivia Teaser 21**
"Rabbit" belongs in Group B because it is a four-legged mammal.

# EVEN MORE CHALLENGES FOR PUZZLE LOVERS!

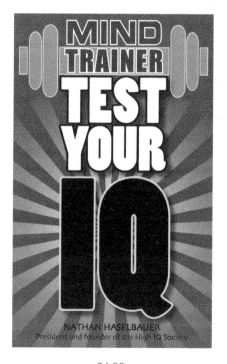

$4.99
ISBN : 978-0-7153-3620-5